W9-BCT-031

2·17·09

Civil
War
Tennessee

Civil War Tennessee

Battles and Leaders

BY THOMAS L. CONNELLY

PUBLISHED IN COOPERATION WITH

The Tennessee Historical Commission

THE UNIVERSITY OF TENNESSEE PRESS

KNOXVILLE

✪ TENNESSEE THREE STAR BOOKS / *Paul H. Bergeron, General Editor*

This series of general-interest books about significant Tennessee topics is sponsored jointly by the Tennessee Historical Commission and the University of Tennessee Press. Inquiries about manuscripts should be addressed to Professor Bergeron, History Department, University of Tennessee, Knoxville. Orders and questions concerning titles in the series should be addressed to the University of Tennessee Press, Knoxville, 37996-0325.

973.7

Library of Congress Cataloging in Publication Data

Connelly, Thomas Lawrence.
  Civil War Tennessee : battles and leaders.

  (Tennessee three star books)
  "Published in cooperation with the Tennessee Historical Commission."
  Bibliography: p.
  Includes index.
  1. Tennessee—History—Civil War, 1861–1865.
2. United States—History—Civil War, 1861–1865—
Campaigns and battles. I. Title. II. Series.
E531.C66   973.7'3'09768   79-14885
ISBN 0-87049-284-5
ISBN 0-87049-261-6 pbk.

ABOUT THE AUTHOR

Twice awarded the Jefferson Davis Award for the best book of the year on the Civil War, Thomas L. Connelly is a native of Nashville and a graduate of Rice University. He is professor of history at the University of South Carolina, book review editor for the *Columbia Record,* and an advisory editor for the *Papers of Jefferson Davis.* Connelly's extensive writings on the Civil War and Southern history include numerous journal articles and reviews. Among his many books are *Army of the Heartland: The Army of Tennessee, 1861–1862; Autumn of Glory: The Army of Tennessee, 1862–1863; Will Success Spoil Jeff Davis;* and *The Marble Man: Robert E. Lee and His Image in American Society.*

Cover Photograph: Detail from Howard Pyle's painting, "The Battle of Nashville," reproduced courtesy of the Minnesota Historical Society.

For Nan and Bob McDill

Contents

ILLUSTRATIONS

Civil
War
Tennessee

1. Tennessee Goes to War

It was done. The torchlit parades, stump orations, and fiery newspaper editorials were a thing of the past. On June 8, 1861, by a vote of over 105,000 to 47,000, Tennesseans formally ratified a resolution of independence. Tennessee was the last state to join the new Confederacy.

The victory for the secessionist camp had been difficult to obtain. For almost five months a bloodless, miniature civil war had been fought in Tennessee between those who chose the old Union and those who joined the rising bloc of supporters of the fledgling Confederacy.

The Unionists had won the first round in February. The secession of South Carolina in December 1860 had tested the convictions of most southern states, and Tennessee was no exception. A referendum was called for February 9, so that the state's citizens could decide whether they wished to call a secession convention, as had sister states to the south.

East Tennessee Unionists such as "Parson" William Brownlow railed against the secession effort. *Brownlow's Knoxville Whig* even suggested that East Tennessee should secede from Tennessee if secession were approved. Brownlow swore that mountain people would never be "hewers of wood" for the slave aristocracy west of the Cumberland Mountains. Far to the west, across the Tennessee River, the cotton planters of West Tennessee urged secession.

The West Tennessee planters were to be disappointed. On February 9, Tennessee voters rejected the proposed call for a secession convention. Even this did not stop some rabid secessionists. Franklin County citizens had voted strongly for the secession convention and were so determined to join the Confederacy that some threatened to secede from Tennessee if the state did not leave the Union. Led by a young Winchester attorney, Peter Turney, the county voted to secede from the Union. Later, in May, 1,200 volunteers under Colonel Turney gathered at Winchester, organized the First Tennessee Regiment, and took railroad cars to Virginia. Turney's group was the first Confederate regiment organized in

Tennessee and would fight in the Army of Northern Virginia until Lee's surrender at Appomattox.

Meanwhile, another prominent leader was working hard to bring the entire state into the Confederacy. In April, Governor Isham G. Harris was angered by President Lincoln's call for troops to suppress the rebellion. Like many border state people, Harris believed that the Lincoln government had no constitutional right to force the new Confederacy to disband. The governor refused Lincoln's call for troops and spoke heatedly of sending Tennessee troops to aid the Confederates.

By late April, Harris was pushing strongly for secession. He pleaded with the state legislature to declare Tennessee an independent state which would ultimately join the Confederacy. Secession fever was now spreading. Confederate flags dotted streets in Nashville and Memphis, and talk on street corners and saloons was of joining forces with Jeff Davis. On May 6 the General Assembly passed "A Declaration of Independence" and called for a public vote on June 8 so that the state's citizens could accept or reject independence.

Obviously the shrewd Isham Harris was after more than independence from the United States. He was manipulating Tennessee into a position where there would be little choice but to join the Confederacy. Relations with the United States government were severed, a large state army was raised, and talk was abundant of a possible invasion by Federal troops. Obviously the voters would grasp that an independent Tennessee could not survive and that the state's security rested with the Confederacy. Also, like Harris, many citizens were angered by Lincoln's April call for troops to put down the rebellion. So Harris worked to place Tennessee as close to the Confederacy as possible, without actually joining the Rebels. On May 7, the day after the legislature declared an independent Tennessee, the state entered into a "military League" with the Confederate government. Tennessee would allow its military forces to be controlled by the Confederacy.

The first week of May produced another significant development. On May 6, the Tennessee legislature passed the army bill, which authorized a large force of 55,000 men, divided into regiments, brigades, and divisions. In July this state army would be transferred to the Confederacy, and it would become the nucleus of the main army on the western front

---

Confederate Governor Isham G. Harris. Courtesy of Tennessee State Library.

—the Army of Tennessee. The Army of Tennessee became the South's chief fighting force in the region between the Mississippi River and the Great Smoky Mountains. Its battle flags bore names such as Fort Donelson, Shiloh, Murfreesboro, Chickamauga, and Atlanta. Just as the state army raised in Virginia became the Army of Northern Virginia, the Tennessee state force evolved into one of the Confederacy's two great armies, with leaders such as Generals Albert Sidney Johnston, P.G.T. Beauregard, and Joseph Johnston.

War fever was in the air during May and June of 1861, as thousands of young Tennesseans flocked to the state colors. The basic unit in the new army was the regiment of about 1,000 men. Regiments were composed of small companies, each formed of men from a single county.

The grim side of war appeared to be far distant in these early months. When regiments gathered at county courthouses for initial organization, they were treated to grandiose oratory by local politicians, baskets of fried chicken prepared by ladies in the community, and the admiring glances of parasol-clad young lasses. The men were then marched off to camps of instruction, which were organized throughout the state.

After being trained, most regiments would remain on the western front, assimilated into what would become the Army of Tennessee. Some, however, went to other war theaters. In the summer of 1861, Virginia appeared to be the area most threatened, and a number of regiments of green volunteers traveled on rickety trains to the eastern front. Other regiments would experience combat in several areas. The Second Tennessee Regiment, commanded by Colonel William Bate, hastened to Virginia in May, was accepted into Confederate service, and fought under General P.G.T. Beauregard at the battle of First Manassas. The Second Tennessee returned to the western front and fought in every major campaign from Murfreesboro to the Army of Tennessee's surrender in 1865. The Third Tennessee Regiment was organized in Knoxville. By June 2, the regiment was in the Virginia theater, fought at First Manassas, and in 1862 returned to East Tennessee. It surrendered in the Vicksburg siege.

Other regiments would venture eastward and never return. Typical was Colonel Robert Hatton's Seventh Tennessee Infantry. Organized in Sumner county in May, the regiment fought in General "Stonewall" Jackson's Shenandoah Valley campaign and with General Robert E. Lee at battles such as the Seven Days, Second Manassas, Fredericksburg, and Gettysburg and at the siege of Richmond and Petersburg. At Appomattox, there were only forty-seven men left to surrender.

But most Tennessee regiments remained in the West and became the backbone of the Army of Tennessee. In July, General Leonidas Polk assumed command of the Confederate Western Department, which included that part of Tennessee west of the Tennessee River. Now the Civil War was to be a real thing for Tennesseans. Only a few weeks earlier, on June 8, the state's voters had ratified a declaration of independence.

Tennessee was out of the old Union, and everyone readied for war. Down in Memphis, a black-bearded former slave trader, Nathan Bedford Forrest, was equipping a regiment of cavalry out of his own pocket. Across the river, at Helena, Arkansas, a young lawyer named Patrick Cleburne was elected colonel for the First Infantry Regiment of Arkansas Volunteers. A former British soldier and a native of County Cork, Ireland, Cleburne would soon lead his men to Nashville. There he would join others such as Felix Zollicoffer, a Nashville newspaper editor who laid down his pen to become a Confederate general.

They were all led by the first commander of the Army of Tennessee, General Leonidas Polk. Polk was a large, impressive man who would become one of the army's most beloved figures. He had attended West Point, where he had become a close friend of a young cadet from Mississippi, Jefferson Davis. Then Polk laid aside the sword to enter the Episcopal ministry and to become a Middle Tennessee planter. A number of members of the Polk family owned huge estates just west of Columbia, on the road to Mt. Pleasant. While operating his plantation, young Leonidas also served as rector of St. Peter's Church in Columbia. By the time the Civil War began, Polk was a well-known clergyman in the South, serving as Episcopal Bishop of the Diocese of Louisiana. Now Bishop Polk laid aside his clerical robes and went to war.

Everyone knew that war would soon come to Tennessee. Kentucky and Tennessee was a geographical bottleneck between the Mississippi River and the Great Smoky Mountains. A Union army could scarcely reach the lower South without marching through the state. For a time in the summer of 1861, the state was protected by Kentucky's proclamation of neutrality which forbade either blue or gray armies in the state. But no one expected this buffer zone to last, and General Polk must ready the state for an invasion.

When the war came to Tennessee, where would it be fought?

UPPER EAST TENNESSEE

It was no surprise that the valley and mountain region of northeastern Tennessee opposed the state's participation in the Confederacy. Northeastern Tennessee, from Knoxville to Kingsport, possessed a deep heritage of being unlike the remainder of the state.

The settlers who migrated to the Great Appalachian Valley north of Knoxville were mainly political and religious dissenters—Scotch-Irish and German. Years of statehood only increased their separatism. Upper East Tennessee had little in common with the state's middle and western counties. Middle and West Tennessee were of the culture of the Mississippi Valley—Democrats and slaveholders, with a more restless spirit, less devotion to the Federal Union.

In contrast, East Tennessee had little of this. People there had few slaves and had a strong love for the Union. Whereas Memphis and Nashville were the state's slave trading centers, a tradition of antislavery developed in the counties northeast of Knoxville.

It was predictable that upper East Tennessee fought hard against secession. In the June referendum, more people in the region voted against secession than voted for the measure in West Tennessee.

The battle was only beginning. Throughout 1861 East Tennesseans rebelled openly against the Confederates. A Greeneville convention attempted the region's secession from Tennessee. Many counties continued to send congressmen to Washington, not to Richmond. By late 1861 well-organized guerilla activity harassed Confederates in the region. Railroad bridges and supply depots were burned, and Confederate sympathizers were terrorized.

By early 1862 the situation was so bad that a brand-new Confederate force of 25,000 men—the Army of East Tennessee—was sent to keep order in the region. The army's commander, General Edmund Kirby Smith, took one good look at pro-Union sentiment and declared, "East Tennessee is an enemy's country."

But the Confederates could not afford to lose upper East Tennessee. Only two railroads joined Confederate armies in Virginia with those of the West, and one of these, the combined lines of the East Tennessee and Virginia and East Tennessee and Georgia railroads, ran from Bristol to Chattanooga. Also, the Shenandoah Valley of Virginia and the Appalachian Valley of East Tennessee were the largest producers of wheat in the Confederacy. Some of the South's richest resources of saltpeter, needed for gunpowder, lay in the cave regions of the Cumberland

East Tennesse Unionists depicted swearing allegiance to the Union in 1861. From *Harper's Weekly.*

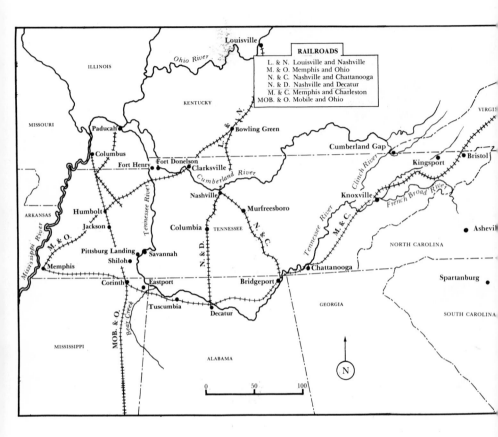

and Unaka ranges. Valuable deposits of lead lay in the Appalachian Valley from southwest Virginia to the Georgia border, while one of the Confederacy's main salt production centers lay just across the Virginia border.

LOWER EAST TENNESSEE

Although the lower valley also contained important wheat resources and the East Tennessee railroad, there were special considerations which made defense of the Chattanooga region critical. East of Cleveland, at the head of the Ocoee River gorge, rich copper deposits were discovered in the 1840s at Ducktown. Ninety percent of the Confederacy's raw copper came from the Ducktown vein. The South needed copper badly, for percussion caps and for casting bronze field artillery.

Even more important was Chattanooga. In 1861 it was a small town of 2,500 inhabitants which had great importance as the rail junction of the upper South. Four critical railroad lines joined there. From Richmond, Virginia, via Knoxville came the East Tennessee route. Here it joined the Nashville and Chattanooga Railroad and the route to Memphis —the Memphis and Charleston—which approached Chattanooga from the west. Then south from Chattanooga, the vital Western and Atlantic Railroad ran to Atlanta.

This was Chattanooga's great importance. It lay along the path of what military historians now refer to as the "Nashville-Chattanooga-Atlanta Corridor." As the war progressed, the Confederates would retreat deeper into the South. By 1863 the South's chief production centers of iron, small arms, artillery, gunpowder, and other necessities would be centered in Georgia and Alabama. Towns such as Columbus, Macon, Augusta, Atlanta, and Selma would be prime Federal targets. Capture this region and the Confederacy would collapse. And it could not be captured without first taking the gateway at Chattanooga.

A long list of Union generals would find that Chattanooga was no easy target. On the north and northeast, the town was shielded by the double range of the Cumberland Mountains and Waldens Ridge. On the west and southwest, in Georgia and Alabama, a series of successive mountain ranges offered protection from an invading army—Sand Mountain, Raccoon Mountain, Lookout Mountain, and several others.

A map of Tennessee's rail network at the beginning of the Civil War.

Nor would it be easy to reach Chattanooga by water. At Chattanooga the Tennessee River left the Great Valley of East Tennessee and roared through a deep gorge west of Chattanooga. The gorge was a maze of whirlpools, sucks, and shoals which extended for forty miles west of the town. Small boats could make it upstream to Chattanooga only with great difficulty. Union gunboats could not reach the city.

LOWER MIDDLE TENNESSEE

Northwest of Chattanooga, on the road to Nashville, lay the important zone of lower Middle Tennessee. This zone consisted of three large river valleys which dominated the 140-mile stretch between Nashville and the Chattanooga fortress—the Stone's, Duck, and Elk River valleys. For two important reasons, Yankee and Rebel armies would fight over this region. Several campaigns of the Army of Tennessee attempted either to protect or to regain control of this war zone, including the battle of Stone's River (December 1862–January 1863), the Duck River campaign (June–July 1863), and the battles of Franklin and Nashville (November–December 1864).

Why was it an important region? One key reason was because these three valleys were one of Tennessee's great breadbaskets. Towns such as Murfreesboro, Shelbyville, Columbia, Winchester, and Manchester were surrounded by very rich limestone-based farmland. In fact, in the total production of corn, hogs, cattle, mules, and horses, the lower Middle Tennessee zone was one of the richest areas in the *entire Confederacy.*

There was another reason why Yankee armies wanted to visit towns such as Columbia and Manchester. The lower Middle Tennessee zone lay squarely in the Nashville-Chattanooga-Atlanta corridor. If the Union army planned to walk to Chattanooga, most likely they would take the main pike which led from Nashville through Murfreesboro to Shelbyville. The road then crossed the Duck and Elk rivers and climbed the Cumberland Mountains at present-day Sewanee, before dropping down to Chattanooga.

If the Union troops came by rail, they would ride rickety box cars

---

(*Above*): A wartime photograph of Chattanooga, with Lookout Mountain in the background. Courtesy of Tennessee State Library. (*Below*): A Federal military photograph of the Cumberland River bridge at Nashville. Courtesy of Brady-Handy Collection, Library of Congress.

pulled by wheezing locomotives down the Nashville and Chattanooga Railroad. The modern Louisville and Nashville Railroad follows the same route General Sherman's bluecoats used in 1864—from Nashville via Murfreesboro, Wartrace, and Tullahoma, then through the long tunnel in the mountains near Sewanee to the Tennessee River.

THE NASHVILLE AREA

When the war began in 1861, everyone knew that Nashville was the prime Federal target in Tennessee. It was the capital, the state's second largest town (17,000 people), and a huge war production center. Except for New Orleans, Nashville was the most cosmopolitan city south of the Ohio River. It boasted such luxuries as a gaslight company, a steam fire department, and an excellent medical college. Nashville could afford such items because it was a wealthy city. Wharves along the Cumberland River bustled with commerce. Prosperous bankers on Union Street did business with large slaveowners in the rich Middle Tennessee bluegrass.

Nashville's socialites lived in large estates on the city's south side. Immense mansions such as Belmont and Rokeby dominated the present-day Hillsboro-Music Row section, while others built fashionable homes out on the Franklin, Hillsboro, and Granny White pikes. Such wealth supported a healthy cultural life. Nashville theaters and opera houses had featured such performers as Edwin Booth, John Drew, Joe Jefferson, and Jenny Lind. In addition, the city boasted five daily newspapers and was well on its way to becoming a major publishing center in the South. Already ten magazines were located in the city, which also boasted the Methodist Publishing House.

In 1861, Nashville became the hub of warfare on the western front. No other western metropolis—even New Orleans—was so vital to the Southern war effort. Nashville was the leading war production center in the West. Factories turned out artillery, small arms, percussion caps for rifles, cartridges, saddles, blankets, and other necessities. Nashville was also the central storehouse for Confederate armies between the Great Smokies and the Mississippi River. Tons of equipment were stored there, from artillery and rifles to tents and uniforms. Warehouses bulged with hundreds of thousands of pounds of foodstuffs collected from the fertile Middle Tennessee region.

There were other reasons why President Abraham Lincoln wished to capture Nashville. The city lay squarely on the route from the Ohio River to Atlanta. From Louisville, the Louisville and Nashville Railroad

led to Nashville, where it linked the railroad to Chattanooga and Atlanta. No army could capture Chattanooga and Atlanta without first
seizing Nashville. Federal armies would also desire the rich Middle Tennessee bluegrass. Nashville was the hub of a fertile agricultural section,
including counties such as Robertson, Wilson, Rutherford, and Wil-
liamson. More than corn and hogs were produced in this region. Northwest of the city, the Confederacy's most important gunpowder mills lay
along the Cumberland River. By the summer of 1861, the State of Tennessee began operating the mills, which shipped gunpowder to armies
throughout Dixie. The Virginia army which won the first victory in the
East at Bull Run used gunpowder from the Cumberland River mills.

THE WESTERN HIGHLAND RIM AREA

There is a narrow strip of land between the Cumberland and Tennessee rivers which separates the Middle Tennessee bluegrass from West
Tennessee's cottonfields and stretches from the Kentucky border to the
front door of Alabama. When the Civil War began, like Nashville, it
was a prime Federal target in Tennessee.

Mr. Lincoln's armies were after two things: iron and waterways. The
land between the rivers was a beautiful, isolated region of high ridges,
fast running streams, waterfalls, and deep ravines. Beneath this fine
scenery were vast deposits of iron ore. Already by 1861, the thirteen-
county region was termed the "Great Western Iron Belt." It was the
South's greatest iron production center. Thousands of slaves and white
laborers toiled at blast furnaces, trip-hammer forges, and foundries in a
vast iron belt of over 5,000 square miles. Millions of pounds of raw iron
were smelted here—iron for rifled muskets, revolvers, swords, artillery,
and a hundred other items.

And through this region coursed two natural invasion routes. The
Cumberland River was navigable for Yankee gunboats from its mouth
on the Ohio River to Nashville. If Nashville fell, the Federals would gain
that city's vast stores, the gunpowder mills upriver, and the Great Western Iron Belt. All of these prizes could be won without seizing the Cumberland River. After leaving Chattanooga, the Tennessee River flows
west across North Alabama and the northeastern tip of Mississippi and
then strikes north across Tennessee to the Ohio River at Paducah. It was
the great route of invasion into the lower South. Gunboats could ascend
the Tennessee River to big Muscle Shoals, near Florence, Alabama. If
the Lincoln gunboats seized control of the Tennessee River, the Confed-

erates would lose Middle Tennessee. Nashville would fall, and the Great Western Iron Belt would have to be abandoned.

THE WEST TENNESSEE AREA

From the Tennessee River to the Mississippi, the vast flatlands of West Tennessee were another prime Federal target in 1861. President Abraham Lincoln considered the recapture of the Mississippi River to be one of the war's great objectives.

Until General Leonidas Polk took charge in July, war preparations in "independent" Tennessee were the responsibility of the energetic Governor Isham Harris and the state commander, General Gideon Pillow. By July their combined efforts had produced a chain of five forts on the Mississippi River. The northernmost outpost was Island Number Ten, which lay in the river at the junction of Tennessee, Kentucky, and Missouri. The Mississippi River made two curious bends here and flowed northward in between. Tennessee authorities fortified Island Number Ten, which lay in the first bend near Tiptonville, Tennessee, while pro-Confederates in Missouri fortified New Madrid in the second bend. South of Island Number Ten, Tennessee authorities built a string of forts. Fort Pillow was built on the First Chickasaw Bluff, near present-day Henning, Tennessee. Ten miles southward, near Covington, powerful river batteries manned the high bluff at Fort Wright. Downstream, six miles above Memphis, the guns of Fort Harris protected the city, as did more artillery on the bluff at the river city. Soon the Confederates added a sixth link to the chain of river forts. On September 3, 1861, General Leonidas Polk's army seized Columbus, Kentucky, just across the state border from Island Number Ten. The high bluff at Columbus became an impregnable fortress, as 140 guns faced north and west across the river.

Such forts shielded more than the river. Memphis, the state's largest city, would be a nice prize for the Federals. The city was the cultural and economic hub for the vast cotton empire of West Tennessee, Arkansas, and the Mississippi Delta. Planters and their wives were eager to escape the heat and boredom of the cottonlands for the social whirl of Memphis. Memphis for them meant lavish balls at the magnificent Gayoso House or equally luxurious meals in the Commercial Hotel dining room which featured calf's-foot jelly, codfish-egg sauce, and roast bear meat. Or a planter could entertain his wife at Crisp's Gaiety Theater which featured famous performers such as Edwin Booth and Charlotte Cushman, or could hear the splendid vocals of Harry Macarthy at Ash's Old Memphis Theater.

Such glitter underlay a wealthy business society in Memphis which, before the war, was founded on valuable cotton, river commerce, and banking interests. The outbreak of war added another element. Next to Nashville, Memphis in 1861 was the most important center of war production and supply in the West. The city's factories and foundries turned out large quantities of small arms, artillery, and other stores.

Yet the river forts could not protect everything. What guarded the vast cotton flatlands stretching east to the Tennessee River? A Yankee army could bypass the forts and Memphis and move from Kentucky along the Mobile and Ohio Railroad, which ran through Union City, Humboldt, and Jackson and eventually to the Gulf of Mexico. And at Jackson, Tennessee, a second rail line offered a clear path to the state capital at Jackson, Mississippi, and eventually to New Orleans.

Obviously, defending Tennessee would be a difficult chore because there were many important areas. Certainly in the summer of 1861, any military man could detect four separate zones which the Federals could be expected to seize. The four prime targets in northern Tennessee were the Mississippi River forts, the land between the rivers, Nashville, and the upper East Tennessee region near Cumberland Gap.

The problem was that until General Leonidas Polk arrived in July, no military man was available to give these four zones adequate attention. Governor Harris was, in effect, commander-in-chief in Tennessee until Polk's arrival. Harris was no professional soldier and was distracted by the task of organizing a state army. Second-in-command in Tennessee was the state army commander, Gideon Pillow. The vain, pompous Pillow was more politician than soldier, and his rank in the Mexican War had been achieved through political connections with President James K. Polk.

The results were disastrous. The Harris-Pillow combination neglected all zones except the Mississippi River forts. One suspects that they overlooked the defense of Middle and East Tennessee because they shared a false sense of security produced by Kentucky's political situation. More experienced military heads could see that Kentucky's neutrality could not last and that eventually Federal armies would occupy that state and invade Tennessee.

Instead, Governor Harris and General Pillow were more concerned with immediate issues. The threat to Tennessee appeared to rest with Union forces in Missouri. After months of internal struggle, the pro-

Union faction appeared to have won Missouri by the early summer. Both men feared that Tennessee would be the target of General Nathaniel Lyon's Union army in Missouri. So Harris and Pillow expended most of their energy in bolstering the defenses on the Mississippi River. Construction began on the chain of forts from Memphis to Island Number Ten. Fifteen thousand state troops were placed there, as was almost all of the state army's artillery and engineers.

Other threatened areas went begging. Only 4,000 troops were garrisoned in all of Middle Tennessee, and the East Tennessee Valley was guarded only by a token force. Worse, construction of defenses to prevent a Union invasion up either the Tennessee or Cumberland waterways was almost neglected. Since the Cumberland River was navigable to Nashville, it would seem imperative that strong fortifications should be erected downstream. In May, Harris had ordered General Andrew Donelson, the new adjutant general of the state army, to select the sites of forts on both the Cumberland and Tennessee rivers. On the Cumberland, Donelson found a suitable location on a high bluff on the west bank, a mile below the village of Dover and seventy-five miles northwest of Nashville.

But work on Fort Donelson was sporadic. Construction proceeded slowly during the summer, and after that Fort Donelson was neglected almost entirely. For a brief time in June, it was manned by forty unarmed men and then was abandoned until October. At that point, a small battery at last was mounted, but no trained artillerists were available, no defenses existed against a land approach, and the fort's garrison numbered a paltry 300 men with inferior weapons or no arms whatever.

The situation at Fort Henry on the Tennessee River was scarcely better. The selection in May of the Fort Henry site was motivated by the lack of a better position near the Kentucky border. By early June, Colonel Adolphus Heiman's Tennessee regiment was given the task of building this fort, which lay only twelve miles west of Fort Donelson on the Cumberland River.

Like Fort Donelson, Fort Henry proved to be a sad commentary on Governor Harris' strategic priorities. The fort's defenses remained unfinished during the summer. Also, the fortress may have been the most poorly designed of any Civil War bastion. It was built on low ground,

General Leonidas Polk, first Confederate commander in Tennessee. Courtesy of Tennessee State Library.

vulnerable to enemy fire from surrounding hills, and was positioned without regard to water levels on the Tennessee River during the rainy winter months. Later, a trained Confederate artillerist visited the fort in September and was shocked at its poor design. Captain Jesse Taylor warned General Polk's headquarters that the fort was not only vulnerable to enemy fire, but that during an ordinary rise of the river, the entire emplacement would be under two feet of water. The neglect of the defense of Middle and East Tennessee continued after Bishop Polk's arrival in July. The reason why Polk was in Tennessee in the first place was because of his interest in protecting the Mississippi River. After war broke out, Bishop Polk hurried to Richmond and urged Jeff Davis to build strong forts from New Orleans to Memphis. Polk also urged Davis to appoint his old West Point roommate, Albert Sidney Johnston, to command the Tennessee frontier. Davis was willing to send the popular Johnston to Tennessee, but that officer had not arrived from California. Would Polk hold temporary command until Johnston arrived? The bishop agreed and soon established headquarters in Memphis. Busy supervising the completion of Island Number Ten and other posts, the good bishop forgot about Nashville and some other places.

Even Polk's limits of command had been shaped by Jefferson Davis to exclude vital parts of Tennessee. Polk's authority as commander of the Western Department extended only to the west bank of the Tennessee River. Until Albert Sidney Johnston's arrival in September, the rest of Tennessee, including Nashville, had no real commander except for Governor Isham Harris.

In September, the military situation changed dramatically in Tennessee. Rumors filtered from telegraph offices out into the streets, saloons, and hotel lobbies—the great Albert Sidney Johnston was coming to Nashville! A large crowd cheered the arrival of the tall, handsome Johnston when his train arrived in Nashville. He made a brief speech at the depot, and then plunged into his new task.

Too much was expected of a man who had become the state's—and the Confederacy's—hero without drawing his sword. Johnston had come from California, where he had commanded the Pacific Department. Federal authorities, who knew of his loyalties, watched him closely and even planned to arrest him if he resigned to fight for Dixie. When Johnston did resign, he slipped out of Los Angeles with a few comrades, dodged pursuing Yankee cavalry, avoided hostile Apaches, and endured blistering heat until they reached El Paso. Eventually Johnston arrived in Richmond, and the news of his daring trek from the Pacific coast had already made him a hero.

On September 10, he had met with Jefferson Davis, and Tennessee had a new commanding general. Johnston was given command of Department Number Two and was now responsible for all Rebel territory from the Great Smokies to the Indian territory. Bands played "Dixie" in Nashville's streets, Confederate flags dotted windows, and the talk was bold in corner saloons. But Johnston knew that the Tennessee frontier was in peril.

One reason for immediate danger was that the Kentucky border was now totally open. On September 3, 1861, Bishop Polk and his second-in-command, the blustery Gideon Pillow, had crossed the state line with a small army and had seized Columbus, Kentucky. When Kentucky's neutrality evaporated, Federal armies poured into the Bluegrass State, and Tennessee was now the prime target. After all, two of President Abraham Lincoln's main war objectives involved invading Tennessee—the seizure of the Mississippi River and the capture of the Nashville-Chattanooga-Atlanta corridor.

Within three months after General Johnston took command in Tennessee, a large number of Federal troops occupied nearby Kentucky. Johnston knew that the Federals had at least 90,000 men in Kentucky, with another 60,000 nearby in Missouri if needed. One army under General Don Carlos Buell was at Louisville, poised to move on Nashville. Another was in western Kentucky under Generals Henry Halleck and Ulysses S. Grant and was expected to test the Mississippi River forts. Johnston was outnumbered three to one, and even some of his best regiments were armed with antiquated muskets, shotguns, or old hunting rifles. His only hope was to concentrate against one line of the enemy's advance into Tennessee. Leaving the river forts with strong garrisons, Johnston should have placed the army at some point in the rear, such as Chattanooga, from which it could have been moved to any part of Tennessee.

Instead, Johnston attempted to defend everything at once. Bishop Polk had the bulk of the Tennessee army in the river forts north of Memphis. Another 5,000 green troops sat in the rain at Forts Henry and Donelson. North of Nashville, at Bowling Green, Kentucky, another miniature army under General William Hardee awaited any Yankee march from Louisville. Far across the state, in the wild Cumberland Mountain country, former Nashville newspaper editor Felix Zollicoffer

---

A contemporary sketch of the war theater in Tennessee. From *Harper's Weekly.*　▶

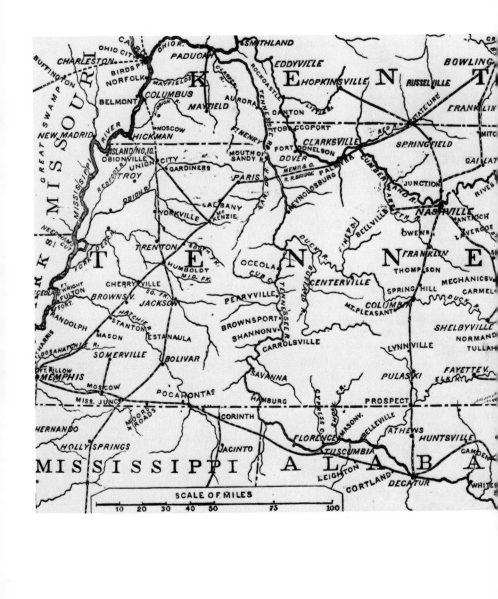

JAMESTOWN
SOMERSET
LONDON
MANCHESTER
WHITESBURY
GLADESVILLE
CUMBERLAND RIVER
K
Y
BARBOURS
MT PLEASANT
LEBANON
ABINGDON
BRISTOL
JONESVILLE
V I R G I N I A
WILLIAMSB.
CUMB. FORD
CUMBERLAND GAP
ESTILLV.
KINGSPORT
BLOUNTSV.
UNION
TAYLOR
SNEEDSVILLE
TAZEWELL
HUNTSVILLE
JACKSONBORO
CLINCH R.
ROGERSVILLE
CARTERS
HOLSTON R.
JONESBORO
ELIZABETH
GAINESBORO
CLEAR R.
EMERY R.
RUTLEDGE
RHEATOWN
RUSSELV.
NEW MARKET
MORRISTOWN
GREENVILLE
LONGMIRES
CLINTON
STRAWBERRY PLAINS
WARLBURG
DANDRIDGE
CEDAR CR.
KNOXVILLE
FRENCH BROAD R.
NEWPORT
BLACK MT
SPARTA
S
KINGSTON
E
TRUNDLES X RDS.
SEVIERV.
E
MARSHALL
LOUDON
MARYSVILLE
ASHEVILLE
MADISONV.
N O R T H
ALTAMONT
MIDWAY
CHILOWEE
WAYNESVILLE
ATHENS
WEBSTER
MILLS RIVER
TELLICO PLS.
C A R O L I N A
HENDERSONVILLE
HARRISON
FRANKLIN
HIAWASSEE R.
VALLEY R.
MURPHY
DUCKTOWN
CHATTANOOGA
HIAWASSEE
CHICKAMAUGA C.
RINGOLD
BLAIRSVILLE
CLAYTON
S O U T H
DALTON
TALULAH FALLS
PICKENS C.H.
PICKENSVILLE
G E O R G I A
CONNESAUGA C.
SAVANNAH
C A R O L
SUMMERV.
DAHLONEGA
MT. YONAH
BELTON
OOSTANAULA R.
CLARKSVILLE
ANDERSON C.H.
CALHOUN
ETOWAH R.

had only 4,000 men to defend East Tennessee. One by one, Johnston's tiny armies were gobbled up. First came Zollicoffer's scarecrow mountain army, many of them armed with flintlock muskets and hog rifles. General George Thomas was a Virginian, disowned by his family when he chose to remain and fight for the old flag. Now he led a small army toward East Tennessee.

Poor Zollicoffer crossed his army to the north bank of the rain-swollen Cumberland River, hoping to keep the Federals out of the East Tennessee area. General George Crittenden had been sent from Richmond by Jeff Davis to replace him. The Kentuckian Crittenden wanted badly to beat the Federals. Foolishly, he ordered an attack on January 19, 1862. A weird fight ensued in the fog and rain near Mill Springs. Zollicoffer was shot down after he accidentally rode into the enemy lines. The flintlock muskets used by many Rebels would not fire in wet weather. Panic gripped the Confederates when it was learned that the beloved Zollicoffer had been killed. When the heavy fog and battle smoke cleared at Mill Springs, the Confederate army had been routed, fleeing into the Tennessee mountains.

With the Confederate right wing gone, the Union forces now moved on the center. Ulysses Grant was a squat, cigar-smoking opinionated fellow who loved good whiskey and getting the job done. In early February, his superior, General Henry Halleck, gave "Sam" Grant 17,000 men, some transports, and seven gunboats. Take the inland rivers, Halleck ordered.

Black smoke hung across the Tennessee River above Fort Henry on the early morning of February 4. The dreaded Lincoln gunboats were coming, and in the morning drizzle they unloaded the bluecoats in the marshy ground north of Fort Henry. General Lloyd Tilghman knew the fight was over, even before it started. Only 2,600 men protected the fort, and most were armed with antiquated muskets used by Andy Jackson's militia in the War of 1812. Worse, the fort was unfinished, and in the cold February rain, water had already lapped over the lower tier of river batteries.

Enough! Tilghman heroically sent his troops overland to Fort Donel-

---

(*Above*): A wartime sketch of Tennessee riflemen en route to the Virginia front in 1861. From *Harper's Weekly*. (*Below*): General Ulysses S. Grant, victor at Fort Donelson, Shiloh, and Chattanooga. Courtesy of Brady-Handy Collection, Library of Congress.

son, while he remained with fifty-six artillerists to provide covering fire. On the afternoon of February 6, Tilghman raised the white flag, and the Tennessee River was open into the lower South.

Terror and dismay obsessed Nashville when the news arrived of Fort Henry's fall. Shopkeepers began boarding up their establishments, crowds began milling in the muddy streets, and lines began to form at railroad ticket offices. Others lined riverfront saloons to brag how Sidney Johnston would soon rout Grant's bully boys. Concern increased when Hardee's Bowling Green force reached Edgefield (present-day East Nashville). Albert Sidney Johnston was stunned by Fort Henry's surrender but more surprised when Grant turned suddenly and marched overland to nearby Fort Donelson.

A curious series of command decisions followed which were responsible in part for the fate of the garrison at Fort Donelson. Even though Johnston on February 7 labeled the fort as "untenable," he began hurrying troops into the garrison. General John Floyd with a Virginia brigade was sent, as were other reinforcements under Gideon Pillow and Simon Buckner. By February 13, the fort's garrison had swelled to 15,000 men.

Why did Johnston send men into the trap at Fort Donelson? A combination of lack of information and his emotional state give the answer. Actually, until the fort's surrender, Johnston was not apprised of the danger from Grant's land force. On the day he described the position as untenable, evidence indicates that he was referring to the Federal gunboats reported to be steaming up the Cumberland. Apparently he never realized that the Confederates could be entrapped by Grant's infantry. For example, when Johnston ordered Pillow's troops into the fort, that officer was instructed to stay as long as possible and then retreat to Nashville.

Until the fort surrendered, Johnston still did not understand how grave the situation was. Generals Floyd and Pillow must share the responsibility because their messages from the fort misled Johnston totally. After gunboat attacks had been beaten off on February 13 and 14, they sent boastful reports which assured that the fort could be held.

Not until the night of February 14 did Floyd and his subordinates realize their peril. Consequently, at dawn on the next day, they launched a

---

The surrender of Fort Donelson, February 16, 1862. From *Harper's Weekly.*

SURRENDER OF FORT DONELSON, FEBRUARY 16, 1862.—[SEE NEXT PAGE.]

violent attack against Grant's right flank, attempting to open the road to Nashville. The attack was successful and the jaws of Grant's trap were opened. At a critical moment, Pillow wavered. He insisted the escape could not succeed, Floyd agreed, and the garrison was marched back into the fortifications. The remarkable thing about the escape attempt was how it was portrayed to Johnston. On February 15, Johnston was informed of a splendid victory over Grant. He was not told that the battle occurred because the trapped garrison was attempting to escape, nor was he told that the plan had failed.

In the early hours of February 16, Johnston was awakened at his Nashville headquarters and was shocked to learn of Fort Donelson's surrender on the preceding night. Suddenly the entire Tennessee line had collapsed. In fact, the process had begun even before Grant captured Fort Donelson. On February 7, Johnston had met at his Bowling Green headquarters with Generals William Hardee and P.G.T. Beauregard. Beauregard had just arrived in the West to serve as second-in-command. The three officers agreed that the Federal seizure of Fort Henry on the Tennessee River made both the Columbus and Bowling Green positions untenable. Beauregard would hasten to the Mississippi River, withdraw Polk's Columbus garrison into West Tennessee, and command independently in that sector until his and Johnston's columns could unite. For his part, Johnston would immediately withdraw Hardee's force of 14,000 troops to Nashville.

Now Nashville must also be lost. With Buell's 50,000 advancing from Louisville toward Bowling Green and Grant only miles downstream on the Cumberland, the city must fall. If Johnston remained there, the Federals would either overwhelm Hardee's command or penetrate up the Tennessee River and cut it off completely from Beauregard. There was no alternative. By the night of February 23, Hardee's rearguard had left the city. The following day, Buell's pickets appeared on the east bank at Edgefield.

The city collapsed in panic. As early as February 16, mobs surged through the streets when the news of Fort Donelson's fate was learned. For days, others jammed roads and rail lines leading southward, desperately hoping to flee to Georgia or Alabama. As Hardee's men retreated through Nashville, the consternation increased. Rioting and looting

General Nathan Bedford Forrest, "Wizard of the Saddle." Courtesy of Tennessee State Library.

gripped the city. On February 18, Colonel Nathan Bedford Forrest arrived with his troops. Forrest, refusing to surrender at Fort Donelson, had escaped through the backwater to Nashville. Even the tough Forrest could not do everything. He did take charge of the awesome task of attempting to salvage some of the army's foodstuffs and military stores, but railroad cars were too few and time was short. As a result, Johnston lost most of his army's stores.

The loss of Middle Tennessee was a disaster for Confederate supply. Gone were the South's chief powder mills on the Cumberland, the Great Western Iron Belt, and the abundant corn and livestock region of Middle Tennessee. Gone as well were tons of supplies at Nashville—bacon, tents, medicine, small arms, uniforms, and many other necessities. Also lost was much of the factory machinery which had made Nashville the center of production on the western front.

There were other losses. Almost a third of Johnston's effective army had been lost at the inland forts and at Mill Springs. Eighty-three pieces of artillery had been given up at Forts Donelson and Henry; 20,000 small arms were seized at Fort Donelson; and at Mill Spring, Crittenden's command had abandoned most of its artillery and small arms.

There was no Confederate army remaining on the western front. Instead, two scattered and isolated detachments under Beauregard and Johnston streamed southward, hopeful of fighting another day.

There was also little Confederate authority remaining in Tennessee. Ironically, it was Governor Isham Harris who in 1861 had labored hard to secure Tennessee's secession. Now, less than a year later, Harris found himself virtually without authority. After the news reached Nashville of the loss of Fort Donelson, the state legislature adjourned hastily to reconvene in Memphis. By earlier authority provided by the legislature, Harris proclaimed Memphis to be the state capital.

Memphis would not boast the state house for long. As the Federals moved against the river town, the legislature on March 20 adjourned, and state officials fled to Mississippi.

Even before the demise of Harris' government at Memphis, a new political order was being established in Tennessee. The staunch East Tennessee Unionist, Senator Andrew Johnson, had refused to follow his state into the Confederacy in 1861 and had retained his seat in Congress.

Andrew Johnson, military governor of Tennessee. Courtesy of Tennessee State Library.

Now Abraham Lincoln appointed Johnson as military governor of Tennessee. Even while General Albert Sidney Johnston's troops marched toward Corinth, Mississippi, Senator Johnson on March 12 arrived in Nashville. Federal authority would never leave the town again.

(*Above*): A wartime photograph of the University of Nashville campus, with Fort Negley in the background. Courtesy of Tennessee State Library. (*Below*): A contemporary sketch of the Federal move against Memphis. From *Harper's Weekly*.

Abingdon Elementary School Library
Abingdon, Virginia

2. The Confederate Resurgence of 1862

The spring thaw came to the high peaks of the Great Smokies and to the rich pungent soil of the Middle Tennessee bluegrass. The cream-colored flowers of Dutchman's breeches and the lush green fields contrasted sharply with the drab prospects of Confederate armies in Tennessee. The collapse of Southern defenses in Middle Tennessee had laid bare the state to invasion by a huge Federal army. On March 11, President Abraham Lincoln had effected a new command whose mission was to seize Tennessee. General Henry Halleck's new Department of the Mississippi boasted over 150,000 combat troops arrayed from Missouri to eastern Kentucky.

In March, without giving the Confederates time to rest, the massive invasion was underway. The spearhead was General Ulysses Grant's Army of the Tennessee, 50,000 strong. By mid-March, Grant's army had pushed up the Tennessee River almost to the Mississippi border and was encamped at Pittsburg Landing, nine miles upriver from Savannah, Tennessee. Grant planned to push into Mississippi but first awaited the arrival of a second army. General Don Carlos Buell's Army of the Ohio, with 50,000 troops, occupied Nashville in late February and was now marching via Columbia and Waynesboro to join Grant. How could the remnants of Albert Sidney Johnston's army withstand a combination of Grant and Buell? And there were more bluecoats. By March, pompous General John Pope was sending another 25,000 Federals against the Mississippi River forts. Meanwhile, another 35,000 of Buell's men not in his field force were held in reserve north of Nashville.

There was no Confederate army to contest these vast forces. Prior to Nashville's capture, Albert Sidney Johnston had divided his Tennessee forces into four miniature armies—Polk's command on the Mississippi River, the garrisons at Forts Henry and Donelson, General William Hardee's army at Bowling Green, and Zollicoffer's troops in East Tennessee. Now two of these four had vanished. The garrisons of Forts

Donelson and Henry were on their way to Federal prisons in the Midwest, and the rout at the battle of Mill Springs had destroyed Zollicoffer's army.

Even the two remaining commands were badly depleted and scattered widely. Beauregard's arrival on the Tennessee front in February prompted a reorganization of Polk's command on the Mississippi River. Until he could join Johnston's column in Mississippi, Beauregard would command independently. He was authorized to abandon Columbus and retreat into West Tennessee, with the eventual goal of joining the troops Johnston brought from Nashville. Unwisely Beauregard split his command. Some 10,000 men would remain to defend Island Number Ten and other garrisons, and only 7,000 followed the Creole to the new concentration point at Corinth, Mississippi. Meanwhile Johnston was bringing only a meager 13,000 troops from the old Nashville-Bowling Green garrison. How could 20,000 Confederates halt Grant's invasion column, much less withstand the combination of Grant and Buell?

But by late March the fortunes of the Confederates were changing rapidly. Almost overnight a new army was created at Corinth. At first it would bear the name Army of the Mississippi but soon would be called the Army of Tennessee. The Army of Tennessee became one of the Confederacy's two greatest armies and was to the west what General Robert E. Lee's Army of Northern Virginia would be to the east—the main hope of the Confederacy.

Much of the credit for this remarkable feat belongs to Johnston's second-in-command, Beauregard. Beauregard's intense personal ambitions now well served the situation. There seems little doubt that his willingness to leave the Virginia theater and serve under Johnston was influenced by private ambitions. In Virginia, Beauregard languished as second-in-command of General Joe Johnston's Army of Northern Virginia. Also, the Creole was too close to Richmond, where he believed his career was being hampered by the machinations of his avowed enemy, Jefferson Davis.

Beauregard received a hero's welcome in Nashville, where almost immediately he confided to a friend in Congress that he was "taking the helm when the ship is already on the breakers . . . ." From their first meeting on February 7 in Nashville, it appears that Beauregard considered Albert Sidney Johnston commander in name only. And within five days, he had succeeded in obtaining Johnston's permission to command independently in the Mississippi Valley.

In effect, Beauregard went to West Tennessee, began organizing a

new army, and invited Johnston to join it. With Bishop Polk's Columbus garrison as a nucleus, Beauregard began building in February what he labeled as the "Army of the Mississippi Valley." Urgent pleas for support were sent to Western governors, the War Department, Beauregard's political allies in Congress, and commanders of neighboring military departments at Pensacola and New Orleans.

Beauregard's ambitions were aided by Albert Sidney Johnston's apparent mental collapse. Grant's unexpected descent on Fort Donelson had shocked Johnston, who by late February appeared confused and unable to make command decisions. It required no West Point education to grasp that concentration of forces on the western front was essential. Yet by February 12, Johnston had informed Beauregard that he was taking Hardee's troops to Chattanooga, and Johnston began preparing for a retreat down the Nashville and Chattanooga Railroad. Had Johnston carried out this strange plan, the two wings of his tiny army would have been some 300 miles apart, with Grant and Buell in between. Only urgent pleas by Beauregard convinced Johnston to abandon the idea and move southwest toward Corinth.

By the time Johnston arrived in Corinth in late March, Beauregard was busy assembling a new army. His success was due in large measure to a combination of weaknesses and strengths in his personality. A propaganda expert was needed both to warn Richmond of the western situation and to talk other commanders into donating men to the cause. The Confederacy had no finer propagandist than Beauregard. Although vain and pompous, Beauregard possessed a gasconade which now proved useful. On any other occasion, his appeal to the Deep South planters to donate plantation bells to be melted down and cast into cannon might appear ridiculous—now it had a good purpose. Always more powerful with the pen than with the sword, Beauregard might appear foppish by signing orders "within hearing of the enemy's guns" or by promising western governors he would march to the Ohio River if they would donate troops—but now such propaganda was needed.

For two reasons Beauregard's pleas for assistance were answered speedily. Few officers in the Confederacy possessed such vast influence in both military and political circles. He had strong political and family ties with influential Louisiana politicians. His command at Fort Sumter

General Albert Sidney Johnston was killed during the battle of Shiloh. Courtesy of Tennessee State Library.

had made him the proverbial darling of South Carolina society. Too, Beauregard's range of Confederate service was unmatched. No other officer commanded the Army of Tennessee, Army of Northern Virginia, and the Carolina Department. In fact, practically every major Confederate general served somewhere during the war under Beauregard's tutelage.

Actually Beauregard's belief in concentration was one element of his frequent disagreements with President Jefferson Davis. Davis, more of an advocate of defending territory than massing forces, had organized the Confederacy in 1861 into a large number of military departments, each defended by an army. The Army of Tennessee, for example, was the military force which protected the Western Department. The problem was that the Federals did not play fair with Davis' policy of dividing the Confederacy into numerous military departments. Time and time again during the war, the Union would concentrate two or even three armies against the Army of Tennessee, while thousands of Confederate troops stood idly by in adjoining military departments.

The situation after the fall of Nashville in February 1862 found three other Confederate departments operating between the Mississippi River and the Great Smokies. Recently Davis had created the Department of East Tennessee to cope with Unionist activity in the region, and General Edmund Kirby Smith's new command "owned" all territory east of the Cumberland Mountains. General Braxton Bragg's Department of Alabama and West Florida defended Mobile and Pensacola, while General Mansfield Lovell's Department Number One protected New Orleans and southern Mississippi.

But the crisis proved too grave for Davis. In March 1862 there occurred one of the few real concentrations of strength which Davis allowed during the war. A combination of Beauregard's persuasive appeals and Richmond's concern resulted in the creation of the new Confederate force at Corinth.

Weeks before Albert Sidney Johnston's arrival in Corinth, the new army was being assembled. General Braxton Bragg was ready to join Beauregard. Although events would later prove that Bragg possessed shortcomings as an army commander, he was an excellent strategist and perceived well the need for concentration. Beauregard even sent an aide to Alabama to plead with Bragg and Governor John Shorter for assistance; at one point Beauregard remarked that he would gladly serve under Bragg rather than be denied his assistance. Such an offer was not needed. When Beauregard's aide arrived in Mobile on February 28, he received a pleasant surprise—Bragg planned to move the following day with practically his entire departmental force of 10,000 men to Beauregard's assistance.

Bragg's arrival on March 2, in advance of his troops, involved far more than the addition of a precious 10,000 troops to the army. Bragg was one of the Confederacy's finest drillmasters, and his regiments, which began arriving at Corinth on March 6, were by far more professional than Beauregard's own troops. Bragg's ten regiments joined others who were gathering at Corinth. From New Orleans, General Mansfield Lovell already had dispatched a brigade from Department Number One. Governor Isham Harris had ordered out state troops in West Tennessee, while several Deep South governors responded to a plea from Beauregard and issued calls for short-term volunteers to meet the crisis.

On March 23, the great concentration was achieved. The last of Johnston's troops had arrived, and now the commanding general joined the new army at Corinth. Quickly that day, the highest level commanders on the western front met in an important conference—the tall, moustached Johnston; the dapper, dark-skinned Beauregard; and the dour, nervous Bragg.

Clearly Beauregard was now in control of the army, though Johnston was commander in title. In fact, Johnston even offered Beauregard formal command of the new army, but the Louisianan refused. Beauregard did not need the command. Both the strategy decisions and army reorganization which came out of the March 23 conference were his doing. The strategy was Napoleonic: concentrate all available forces at Corinth, march to Pittsburg Landing, and strike Grant's army there before it was joined by Buell's column. And to make the concentration greater, Johnston agreed to another Beauregard proposal. Since late February, Beauregard had sought the use of 20,000 troops under General Earl Van Dorn in Johnston's Trans-Mississippi District. On March 23, Johnston telegraphed Van Dorn at Little Rock, Arkansas to cross the river at Memphis and rush his troops to Corinth as soon as possible. Van Dorn left his army behind and hurried to confer with Johnston on April 1.

From the March 23 conference came as well a new organization. For the first time in the war, the western front now possessed a genuine army. True, it was an army in the rough. Practically all of Johnston's men were green troops yet to experience combat. Discipline was a problem, particularly in Polk's command brought from Columbus, Kentucky. Thousands of small arms had been lost in the debacles of the inland forts, Nashville's surrender, and the battle at Mill Springs. At least 150 pieces of artillery had been abandoned or surrendered on the Tennessee front. And the loss of Nashville meant grave shortages of almost everything which an army required—beef and bacon, flour, gunpowder, cartridges, medicine, and other essentials.

What actually happened was little short of remarkable. Between the March 23 conference and the army's move on April 3 against Grant, an army was fashioned out of the conglomerate of scattered regiments and brigades which had been rushed to Corinth. On March 29, under Johnston's signature, the orders were published announcing the new army organization. Actually, Beauregard drew up the plans, and Johnston agreed to them without change.

The new Army of the Mississippi boasted an impressive organization, at least on paper. Johnston remained as commander, Beauregard functioned as second-in-command, and Bragg was appointed chief of staff. The first corps was led by the army's senior commander, General Leonidas Polk. Although he was already proving to be both stubborn and quarrelsome, Polk had both command experience and the confidence of the troops he brought from Columbus. Another corps was assigned to General William Hardee, who had commanded Johnston's center in the Bowling Green-Nashville region. The Georgia-born Hardee, dubbed "Old Reliable" by his troops, was the army's foremost scholar-soldier. A former commandant of cadets at West Point, Hardee had authored *Rifle and Light Infantry Tactics,* the standard textbook still used in 1861 at the Academy. Another corps was given to Chief of Staff Bragg. A Mexican War hero and former Louisiana planter, Bragg came with a year's experience in commanding the Gulf Coast region from Pensacola to Mobile.

In addition, there was a smaller reserve corps assigned to Johnston's former East Tennessee commander, General George Crittenden. The fate of this unit in subsequent days underscored the hasty nature of the army's new organization. Two days after he was assigned to command, Crittenden was unceremoniously relieved when he was found drunk at his headquarters. So less than four days before the army left Corinth to attack Grant, the corps was assigned a new leader—General John C. Breckinridge. Breckinridge's appointment was more political than military. He was no soldier, but he had been a United States senator, vice president in the James Buchanan administration, and a presidential candidate in 1860.

There was no time for this new organization to take shape. On the night of April 2, Johnston and Beauregard discovered they could not wait for Van Dorn's precious 20,000 reinforcements. For days, Buell's army had remained forty miles south of Nashville, slowly preparing bridges to cross the deep, swift Duck River at Columbia. But was Buell actually marching to join Grant? The road forked at Columbia. Buell could march directly into northern Alabama, seize the Memphis and Charleston Railroad, and outflank Johnston's force at Corinth. Or he could move some 100 miles southwest, via Waynesboro, and join Grant on the Tennessee River. For days in late March, Johnston's scouts on the Duck River were unsure of Buell's designs. But on the night of April 2, definite information arrived in Corinth. Buell was marching to join Grant. There was no time to wait for Van Dorn's Arkansas army.

The next three days became a nightmare of ill-fated marching orders, countermarches, and command tangles. Early on the morning of April 3, Johnston continued his policy of allowing Beauregard to direct the army's affairs. Beauregard responded with marching and battle orders totally unsuited to the newness of the army's organization.

Confederate intelligence knew that Grant had moved the bulk of his army from Savannah a few miles upstream to Pittsburg Landing, on the west bank of the Tennessee. Five divisions (about 37,000 troops) under the immediate command of Sherman were encamped on the high sandy bluff overlooking the river landing. Four miles downriver, General Lew Wallace's division rested at Crump's Landing. Beauregard's battle plan, drawn on a table-top on the morning of April 3, called for a surprise attack on the bulk of Grant's army at Pittsburg Landing. Marching on parallel roads from Corinth, the three main corps would rendezvous on the night of April 3 at a road junction called Mickey's, seven miles from the river landing. Then the Confederates would deploy into battle line and attack at dawn on April 4—time enough for victory before Buell's army arrived.

Well enough, but the loose ends of Beauregard's visionary planning on April 3 proved the army's undoing. The Special Order Number Eight, which described the march and battle plan, contained grave flaws which became apparent during the next three days. Several routes would be used to move the short distance to Pittsburg Landing—the Ridge, Monterey-Purdy, and Monterey-Savannah roads. Because the roads often crisscrossed, Johnston's army could reach Mickey's by dawn of April 4 only by the most intricate of timing. Nor did the marching plans consider weather and terrain. It had been raining north of Corinth for several days, and the country was a quagmire of miry roads, flooded

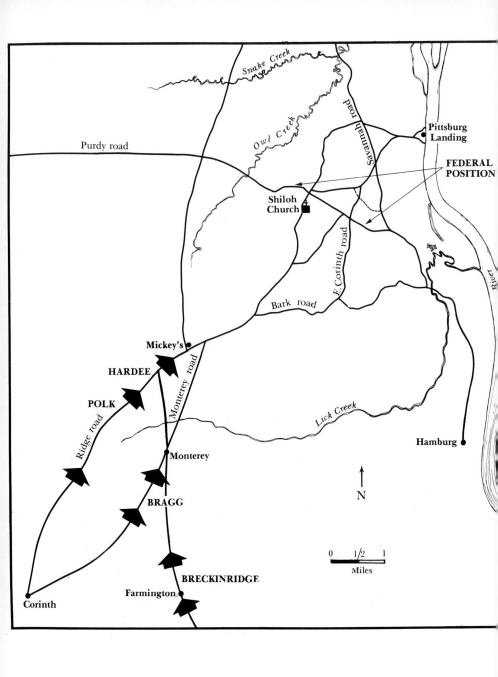

swamps and gullies, and soggy, dense forest. Such conditions made it almost impossible to move wagons and artillery.

The battle plans were equally unrealistic. According to Beauregard's grand design of April 3, the army was to rendezvous at Mickey's junction sometime that night and would attack Grant's position at dawn. The plan of attack, however, promised only confusion. Instead of allotting the three main corps—Polk, Bragg, and Hardee—a portion of the battlefield, Beauregard decided upon an attack by successive corps. Confederate intelligence had placed Grant's army within a three-mile wide region, bounded on the east by Lick Creek and on the west by Owl Creek. Hardee's corps was to attack at dawn, spread along this three-mile front, and would be followed by successive attacks mounted by Bragg, Polk, and finally the reserve troops under Breckinridge. Such a plan invited only confusion, particularly in the broken, dense terrain surrounding Pittsburg Landing. The corps were to move forward only 1,000 yards apart; it required no seer to predict that soon they would become entangled.

Another critical matter was evident in Beauregard's plan of April 3. What was the purpose of the attack? There is considerable evidence to support the thesis that, in the haste of that day's preparations and the confusion of the next two days, Johnston and Beauregard had in mind different objectives. The battle orders of April 3 (issued under Johnston's name) stated that the objective was to strike hard at Grant's left flank near the Tennessee River, drive his troops away from the river landing, and force them back on Owl Creek. But when Beauregard penned his official report after the battle, he did not mention this aim but described the plan as the opposite—that Grant would be driven back into the Tennessee River.

Whatever the real Confederate objective, it was lost in chaos even before the army left Corinth. There would be no morning attack on April 4. The largest Confederate army ever assembled in the West was an unwieldy mass of young, inexperienced troops whose officers were little better. The muddy streets were filled with swearing teamsters urging on mules and with confused regimental leaders stalled in a massive traffic jam. By nightfall, Bishop Polk's corps was yet to leave Corinth.

Matters became worse on April 4. The roads to Pittsburg Landing be-

---

The route of the Confederate advance prior to the battle of Shiloh. From James Lee McDonough, *Shiloh—in Hell before Night.*

came a sea of mud afloat with heavy wagons and cumbersome artillery. Because the several roads crisscrossed, intersection points became impossible tangles, and whole corps waited for hours for others to clear the road. Bragg's and Polk's corps became caught in an almost hopeless snarl, and the green troops became more nervous. It was raining. What if their rifled muskets did not fire? Remember Zollicoffer's men at Mill Springs—how their powder became wet, and they angrily dashed their useless weapons across fence posts. So the troops bound for the Shiloh bloodbath decided to test fire their weapons, but officers frantically begged them to cease firing, lest Grant's men know of their approach.

April 4: by nightfall, only Hardee's corps had reached the staging area at Mickey's junction, and a frustrated Albert Sidney Johnston exclaimed "This is puerile. This is not war!" There would be no attack on April 4.

Nor would they fight on April 5. The closer they marched to Pittsburg Landing, the worse the muddy roads became. Now they were little more than forest trails slashed through a morass of ravines, swamps, and thickets. There was more test firing of weapons, and now there was also hunger. Inexperienced marchers rarely conserve their food, and some regiments had gobbled down their soggy biscuits and raw bacon within a day after leaving Corinth.

The Prussian military theorist von Clausewitz once observed that there were times when an army becomes weary and works against its leader. The momentum slows, and only the general's determination forces the issue. Such appeared the case late on the afternoon of April 5, when the army's high command met for a conference near Mickey's. As Bragg, Polk, Johnston, Breckinridge, and Beauregard stood by a roadside fire, nerves and tempers were frayed. Beauregard, supported by Bragg, argued that the army should retreat to Corinth. The central element in the Creole's battle plans had been the concept of a surprise attack —a quick overland march on the afternoon of April 3, followed by a lightning assault. Now, Beauregard protested that a surprise attack was impossible. Surely a three-day Confederate march could not go undetected. Already there had been clashes between Union reconnaissance forces and Johnston's advance units. And on April 5, many Confederate troops, tense because of the bad weather and the delay, had fired their guns to test them. Surely Grant must be strongly entrenched in the wilderness ahead.

For weeks Johnston had been commander in title only and had willingly allowed Beauregard to dominate top-level decisions. This time it would be different. At stake was the possible defeat of Grant before the dreaded concentration with Buell was a reality. Johnston must have known as well that the prize of a victory over Grant was the regaining of precious territory in Tennessee. If Grant's army were crushed, Federals on the Mississippi River surely must retreat. And Buell no doubt would withdraw to Nashville, and perhaps even into Kentucky. The prospects were worth the risk. The high command debated as the evening drizzle played havoc with the roadside fire, but Johnston was determined. At the conference's ending, he announced calmly that the army would attack at daylight.

Still this scenario did not quiet Beauregard's fears. At dawn, there was another council of war at Johnston's headquarters. As the generals huddled around a small fire, Beauregard again insisted that the Confederates should retire to Corinth. Even as the argument continued, skirmish fire broke out on Hardee's front. Now the question was indeed moot. Johnston murmured, "the battle has opened, gentlemen." It was now five o'clock in the morning, and Hardee's advance had struck a reconnaissance force from General Benjamin Prentiss' division in the Union center. Within an hour, Hardee's main line had struck like an avalanche, and by seven o'clock both Sherman's and Prentiss' camps had been overrun.

Clearly Beauregard's fears had been unfounded. Never before or again in the Civil War had an army so completely surprised another. After the war, Grant, Sherman, and others would feebly attempt to explain why the Confederate attack was a surprise. After all, for at least two weeks Union intelligence sources had warned of a concentration at Corinth. And certainly after April 4, Grant and Sherman—his immediate commander at Pittsburg Landing—should have been on guard. On April 5 the picket line of the Seventy-second Ohio Regiment encountered Rebel cavalry in force and had contact with infantry and artillery units as well. That same afternoon, a Federal colonel warned Sherman that a large enemy force was approaching. An angry Sherman only rebuked him strongly.

Flush with the successes already gained in Tennessee, Grant and his officers had little respect for the Confederates and were totally overconfident. On April 5, the very day that the Southern army drew near to the Shiloh field, Sherman informed Grant that he did not expect to be attacked, and Grant telegraphed the same opinion to Washington.

It was early in the morning on Sunday, April 6, and a bright sun was slowly beginning to dry out the rain-soaked forests around the river landing. Many bluecoats were still asleep or lounged in camp, totally unaware that 40,000 Confederates were a half-mile away.

There was one officer in Prentiss' division, Colonel Everett Peabody, who was uneasy about the reports of Rebel activity near his lines. So before dawn, Colonel Peabody sent out three companies of Missouri infantry to reconnoiter the roads leading toward Corinth. Shortly after it was light enough to see, the Missouri troops, all new recruits, reached an open field owned by a local farmer named Fraley. At five o'clock in the morning the Missourians encountered the advance of Hardee's corps, and the greatest battle yet fought in North America began.

Within two hours the camps of Prentiss and Sherman had been swept away in the onslaught of the surprise attack. In fact, Grant's only salvation that morning was uncertainty in the Confederate high command. Even as Hardee's skirmishers opened fire, Johnston and Beauregard debated again the Creole's suggestion that the element of surprise was lost and that the army must retreat. No retreat. Already the guns had opened. Enthused by the developing surprise attack, Albert Sidney Johnston urged his horse forward toward the front lines. En route he ran across his friend from the old army days in Utah, Colonel John Marmaduke. Watching Marmaduke's Arkansas troops press forward, Johnston placed his hand on his friend's shoulder and murmured, "My son, we must this day conquer or perish!"

Conquering would be a difficult task despite the Confederate advantage of surprise. Even in the dawn hours of the battle, the top-level direction of the attack became a haphazard affair. Johnston's ride to the front lines took him out of overall battle direction. Through the morning he behaved more like a war correspondent or front line observer than a battle commander. By mutual agreement, Beauregard was to remain in the rear and send reinforcements forward. From this position, the Creole had far more control over the nature of the assault than did Johnston.

And Beauregard's control worked against Johnston's plan to strike Grant's left flank and drive the Federals away from their base at the steamboat landing. Instead, Beauregard directed reinforcements forward to achieve his own aim—to force the bluecoats into the Tennessee River. Confederate power was thrust toward the left and center, far from the river. For example, when Polk's and Breckinridge's corps reached the field, Beauregard ordered them to march toward the sound of the most severe fighting, which was on the Confederate left and center.

Even had the top Rebel brass agreed on attack plans, other matters soon reduced the operation to an isolated series of encounters. With Beauregard busy in the rear sending reinforcements forward and with Johnston absent on the front lines, the attack had almost no direction. Whole brigades wandered to the front aimlessly. Typical was a situation which occurred on the critical right flank near Lick Creek, where Johnston had planned the real assault. Colonel George Maney's crack First Tennessee Infantry and Bedford Forrest's cavalry had been posted there early in the morning, and frankly were forgotten. Shortly before noon, still without any orders, Maney and Forrest, on their own initiative, moved to the front.

Even the army's initial alignment worked against Johnston's plans. The dense thickets, ravines, and swamps hid Grant's battle line. Although he planned a dawn attack, Johnston did not order an engineer officer to reconnoiter the enemy's left flank on the river until four o'clock that morning, and the report was not received until almost six hours after the battle had started.

Without reconnaissance, Johnston's battle line was arranged in a manner which would make it difficult to drive the Federals from the river. The main Union line extended along a three-mile front between Owl Creek on the west and Lick Creek on the east. Sherman's division was posted between Owl Creek and the Corinth-Pittsburg Landing Road. Prentiss' division lay east of the road, occupying the center. The Federal left consisted only of a single detached brigade led by Colonel David Stuart, on some heavily timbered bluffs near Lick Creek. In brief, Sherman's and Prentiss' line extended in a northwest-southeast line across the Corinth-Pittsburg Landing Road, and then bent sharply to the northeast in Stuart's position near the river. Johnston's battle line was also formed in a northeast-southwest fashion. This meant that the planned surprise attack would strike first the Union right and center—not the critical left flank. Not until ten o'clock in the morning—five hours after the battle had opened—would the weak Federal left near the river be under fire.

By 9:30 A.M. Johnston had received the reconnaissance report which told of the weakness of the enemy left flank on the river. Even now, the opportunity to smash the Federal left was not used to full advantage. The Federal center under Prentiss proved stubborn to drive back. In the late morning Prentiss withdrew his men to an old wagon road east of the Corinth-Pittsburg Landing Road. This wagon trace, known later as the Sunken Road, with its "Hornet's Nest" at the north end, provided enough natural protection to slow Johnston's assault.

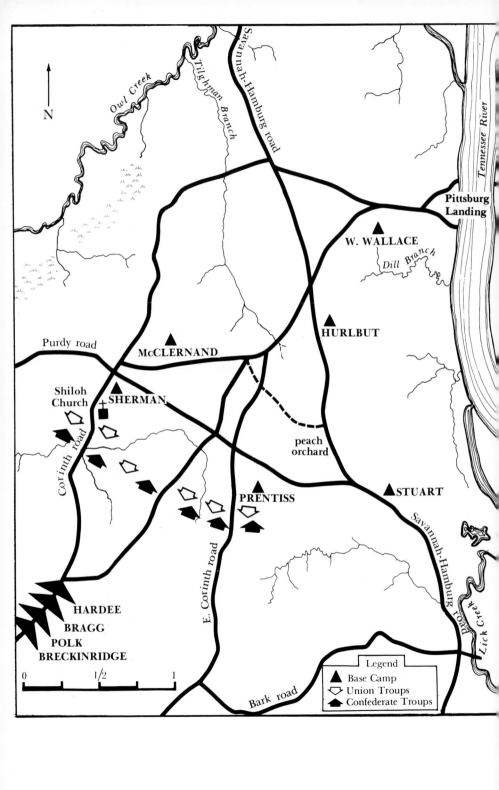

Worse, Prentiss' stubborn defense of the "Hornet's Nest" almost made the Confederates forget the battle's objective. When Johnston learned of the weakness of the Union left near the river, he rode to the area and shortly after 10 A.M. ordered some brigades from Breckinridge's reserve corps to begin an attack. This was more easily commanded than accomplished; the woody ravines and dense thickets afforded Stuart's brigade ample protection. Not enough force was applied to dislodge Stuart and open the road to the river landing.

Instead, during the late morning of April 6, the Confederate high command became involved in an attempt to dislodge Prentiss from his position along the Hornet's Nest. Hindsight has taught that Johnston's army should have bypassed the position and concentrated upon the weakness of the Federal right and left flanks. Instead, during the midday, eleven assaults were sent against Prentiss' position. By drawing Johnston's attention from the river flank, Prentiss bought precious time for Grant to reform a battle line near the river landing. Not until about 5:30 P.M. did Prentiss hoist the white flag, surrendering some 2,200 men who had given their comrades time enough to regroup in the rear.

By then the battle complexion had changed markedly. During the early afternoon, Albert Sidney Johnston had moved to the weak Federal left to supervise the attack by Breckinridge's reserve corps. Shortly after two o'clock he was struck below his right knee by a musket ball. Why Johnston failed to notice the wound immediately is uncertain. Ironically, only a short time before, Johnston had dispatched his staff surgeon to care for wounded Federal prisoners, and now he literally bled to death in the saddle from an arterial wound. Johnston collapsed, and his volunteer aide, Governor Isham Harris, sought frantically to locate the wound. It was too late. By 2:30 the Confederate commander in the West was dead.

Now the command went to Beauregard. For weeks the Louisianan had been hampered by a recurring throat ailment and may have been unable to provide the best command direction. Certainly he did not grasp the vulnerability of the weak Yankee left flank and thus only continued the attacks against the Hornet's Nest.

Finally, about 5:30 P.M., the white flag was raised along the Sunken Road. Prentiss' surrender was a Pyrrhic victory for the Confederates.

The battlefield at Shiloh. From McDonough, *Shiloh—in Hell before Night.*

While Prentiss had slowed the Rebel advance, Grant had established a new battle line at the river landing. A mass of siege guns was planted atop the bluff above the landing, and the weary Confederates could not take the position. Until nightfall, Beauregard's men charged the steep bluffs but were driven back by the massed siege artillery, aided by fire from Union gunboats in the Tennessee River. Finally, some time after six o'clock, Beauregard halted the attack for the day.

From the standpoint of what Beauregard knew, it was a wise decision. His troops were exhausted and lacked the power to overrun Grant's new position. They were also out of control. Whole regiments and brigades were missing, having straggled in the rear to plunder hams, tobacco, and other booty in captured Yankee camps. Thousands more were actually lost from their commands, wandering in the tangle of ravines, gullies, and thickets near the river landing.

Too, Confederate intelligence showed that Grant would be easy prey on the morning of April 7. One report indicated that Buell was not marching to join Grant but was moving into northern Alabama; another report predicted that the junction would be made but would not be achieved before Grant had been destroyed. Certainly Beauregard and other ranking officers believed that Grant must face them on the next morning without Buell. That night the Creole telegraphed Richmond of the "complete victory" achieved, while Braxton Bragg wrote his wife that Grant would be routed on the next morning.

Actually, Grant was already receiving reinforcements which would reverse the situation within hours. General William Nelson's division had reached nearby Savannah on April 5, and Buell himself was there that evening. And by twilight of April 6, Nelson's lead brigade had reached the west bank of the river at Pittsburg Landing. These reinforcements, together with the arrival of General Lew Wallace's division from nearby Crump's Landing, reversed the initiative of the battle. By dawn of April 7, Grant already had 13,000 fresh men for another day's battle, and by late afternoon, when all of Buell's and Wallace's men were up, he would have twice that number.

So affairs on April 7 became only a matter of time. Shortly after dawn, it was now Grant who stalked the Confederates rather than the reverse. Until late afternoon Beauregard's men fought back gamely, but the Yankee reinforcements proved to be too strong. Shortly after four o'clock, Beauregard sadly ordered a retreat to Corinth.

It was the bloodiest engagement of the war yet. Almost 24,000 men had been killed, wounded or captured—more men than the Confederates had on the field at Bull Run in 1861. Rebel losses were especially costly. The 11,000 losses meant that almost one in every four Confederates at Shiloh was a casualty.

The disaster was far larger than the misery of Shiloh. Within two months, the entire chain of Confederate forts on the Mississippi River had been surrendered or abandoned. When Beauregard gave up his Columbus position, Southern hopes rested with General John McCown's 8,500 troops in the fortresses of New Madrid, on the Missouri shore, and Island Number Ten. In early March, General John Pope with 25,000 men marched against these forts. McCown's defense of New Madrid was feeble. After Pope attacked on March 12, McCown abandoned the position on the following day, sending part of his garrison to Island Number Ten. Disgusted with McCown's performance, Beauregard replaced him with General W.W. Mackall, who now attempted to stem Pope's advance on Island Number Ten. Mackall's garrison, outnumbered more than three-to-one by Pope's invaders, fought stubbornly. But Flag Officer Andrew Foote's squadron, Pope's numbers, and dwindling supplies proved decisive. Island Number Ten became a trap, and Confederate losses were heavy. On April 7, Mackall surrendered 7,000 men, 158 pieces of artillery, and 7,000 small arms. The seizure of other Confederate forts on the Tennessee portion of the Mississippi River was only a matter of time. On June 4, Fort Pillow and Fort Randolph were abandoned, and the way was open for the capture of Memphis.

By the evening of June 6, 1862, all of Tennessee west of the Cumberland Mountains was in Federal hands. The last position to fall was Memphis. It was protected only by a handful of Confederate troops and by a river fleet of eight steamboats which had been converted into warships. Flag Officer Andrew Foote, still suffering from wounds received in the engagement at Fort Donelson, had been replaced by Flag Officer Charles Davis. After securing Fort Pillow, Davis steamed downriver to Memphis with a strong fleet of five gunboats and four supporting rams. On June 6, several thousand residents lined the bluffs at Memphis to view the naval battle. Within two hours, all but one ship in the Confederate fleet had been sunk or captured. A small rowboat with a flag of truce reached the Tennessee shore, the mayor surrendered the town, and immediately a Union flag was raised over the Memphis post office.

Now the Confederate situation in the West appeared even more desperate than it had been before the Shiloh bloodbath. All of Tennessee was in enemy hands except for the East Tennessee Valley. Some 20,000 more Confederates had been lost at Shiloh and in the struggle for the

Mississippi River. Worse, the dreaded junction of Grant's and Buell's armies was now a reality. General Henry Halleck came in person to Pittsburg Landing to direct a new campaign against Beauregard's shattered army. On April 29, Halleck marched against Corinth with a huge army group of 125,000 men. Sickness and battle losses had so depleted Beauregard's army that he could muster less than a fourth that number. On May 30 Corinth was abandoned, and Beauregard fell back deeper into Mississippi. Three weeks later President Jefferson Davis, angered at Beauregard's performance, removed the Creole from command on the western front.

Within weeks, Confederate hopes lifted on that front. Much has been written—mostly unfavorable—of Beauregard's successor, General Braxton Bragg, who would command the Army of Tennessee longer than would any other officer. Nervous, argumentative, and quick to blame others, Bragg proved ill-suited for army command. But he was a masterful strategist, one of the best which the Confederacy possessed. Bragg understood well that the war could be won or lost in the West. He was a disciple of the Beauregard school of strategy—that Western Confederates must be concentrated against a single line of the enemy's advance.

Now Halleck gave Bragg such an opportunity. Since 1861 the Lincoln administration had espoused three main strategic objectives: capture Richmond, gain the Mississippi Valley, and seize the Nashville-Atlanta corridor. The latter two were the responsibility of Halleck in the summer of 1862. So he divided his huge army group after seizing Corinth. In June, Buell's army was directed to move eastward across northern Alabama and capture Chattanooga. Meanwhile, Grant would operate from West Tennessee against the Rebel stronghold at Vicksburg.

Exactly who fashioned the strategy of uniting forces against Buell's column is unclear. Certainly Beauregard, after his removal from command, urged Bragg to do so. Bragg favored the prospect, as did the commander in East Tennessee, General Edmund Kirby Smith. Kirby Smith continually urged Bragg to move his army to East Tennessee and combine forces. To convince Bragg, Smith dangled the prospect of an invasion of Kentucky.

(*Above*): A sketch of the naval battle prior to the surrender of Memphis. From *Harper's Weekly*. (*Below*): Cumberland Gap, a strategic point on the border between Tennessee, Kentucky, and Virginia. From *Harper's Weekly*.

What was developing was the greatest offensive ever undertaken by Confederates on the western front. The catalyst for this counteroffensive was Kentucky. President Jefferson Davis, a Kentuckian, had always believed that his native state was pro-Confederate and should be liberated. Davis in turn was influenced by prominent Kentucky officers such as the dashing cavalryman, General John Hunt Morgan. A June raid by Morgan's men into Kentucky excited the Confederate populace and demonstrated the weakness of Federal defenses in the bluegrass. Within a week after leaving East Tennessee, Morgan's column had reached the outskirts of the state capital at Frankfort, capturing Yankee garrisons and vast stores in its wake. The Federal command in the state almost collapsed, and a disgusted Abraham Lincoln remarked "they are having a stampede in Kentucky."

Morgan's raid whetted Confederate ambitions to gain Kentucky, and the cavalryman reported that the entire state would rise up against the Federals if Bragg and Kirby Smith would come. Invasion fever swept the western front by July. Certainly Tennessee could be regained, and perhaps the Stars and Bars would float on the Ohio River. It appeared that by mid-summer the initiative in the West had passed to the Confederates.

Much of the credit for this change of initiative—and for stalling Buell's advance—belonged to Bragg's cavalry. Not until 1863 would horsemen on the western front be organized into a separate cavalry corps. Until then, they would operate in brigade and division strength against Union communications. The fate of Buell's advance on Chattanooga became a textbook exercise in the proper use of cavalry. Three separate cavalry raids—two into Tennessee—stalled Buell's advance. In early July, Colonel Frank Armstrong's cavalry stormed into North Alabama and wrecked part of Buell's intended supply line along the Memphis and Charleston Railroad. Undaunted, Buell shifted his line of supply to the Nashville and Chattanooga Railroad.

Generals Nathan Bedford Forrest and John Morgan now proceeded to demolish Buell's line of communication. On July 13, Forrest and some 1,000 troopers swooped down from the Cumberland Mountains and captured Murfreesboro. Forrest bagged General Thomas Crittenden, 1,200 prisoners, and a quarter of a million dollars worth of Yankee stores. More important, Forrest's troopers burned the Nashville and Chattanooga Railroad bridges over Stone's River, shutting down Buell's supply line for two weeks.

The Kentuckian John Morgan did even better. On August 12, Morgan and his cavalrymen stormed Gallatin, destroyed a large section of track on the Louisville and Nashville Railroad, and demolished an 800-foot tunnel north of the town. Now the supply line to Louisville would be closed for months.

By mid-August, the combined raids of Armstrong, Forrest, and Morgan had wrecked Buell's offensive. Desperate, the Federal general massed the bulk of his cavalry under General R.W. Johnson and sent it to Middle Tennessee to drive out the troublesome Morgan. Suddenly there was the question of who was the hunter and the hunted. Morgan bushwhacked Johnson west of Hartsville, and the Federal advance became an embarrassing rout. The "Hartsville Races" continued through an afternoon, as Johnson's horsemen fled wildly for the protection of the Cumberland River. When the day ended, Buell's cavalry was scattered badly, and Johnson and his staff were prisoners. It was enough for Buell; by late August, he abandoned his move on Chattanooga and fell back into Middle Tennessee.

Never again in the Civil War did the Confederacy possess the momentum present in August and September of 1862. On the eastern front, General Robert E. Lee's spectacular victories in the Seven Days and Second Manassas campaigns had turned the war around in that sector. By early September it was Lee, not General George McClellan, who was the invader, as the Virginia army marched into Maryland.

Confederates in the West were also on the march. On July 23, Braxton Bragg began shifting his army from the Mississippi front to join Kirby Smith at Chattanooga. Now the Confederates effected a Napoleonic concentration against Buell. Within almost a week, Bragg shifted 35,000 troops to Chattanooga. The route was a long one, since the Memphis and Charleston Railroad in northern Alabama remained in Federal hands. Instead, Bragg's men went via rail to Mobile; then by ferry, steamboat, and rail to Montgomery; and thence by rail to Atlanta and Chattanooga. On July 27, the first of Bragg's regiments reached the Tennessee front. Four days later, Bragg and Kirby Smith met to plan the grand offensive.

Yet the Chattanooga meeting left two important matters unsettled. Who would command? Bragg outranked the younger Kirby Smith, but both men commanded military departments. It was apparent that Kirby Smith was in no hurry to defer to Bragg's senior position, and Jefferson Davis did little to clear the matter. Instead of designating one general as commander, Davis spoke merely of the hope for "cordial co-operation" between the two generals.

Nor did the Chattanooga conference produce any clear-cut plan for the campaign. Everything seemed to depend upon circumstance. Kirby Smith's army, reinforced by some troops obtained from Bragg, would march from Knoxville against the Union fortress at Cumberland Gap— the gateway to the Kentucky bluegrass. If Kirby Smith's 19,000 troops could dislodge the Federal division posted at the gap, they would be in position either to invade Kentucky or to unite with Bragg. Bragg meanwhile would move with 26,000 troops from Chattanooga into Middle Tennessee.

Within a few days after their meeting, Bragg and Kirby Smith revised the invasion plans. Now both armies would strike northward into Kentucky. While Kirby Smith moved via Cumberland Gap, Bragg would bypass Nashville and march into central Kentucky. Once in the Bluegrass State, the two Confederate armies would unite under Bragg, the senior officer.

By late August the plan had become even more ambitious, but it was also appearing to be unwieldy. Bragg had left behind in Mississippi some 30,000 troops in two small armies led by Generals Earl Van Dorn and Sterling Price, and Bragg sent orders at the end of the month for the two columns to prevent Grant from reinforcing Buell. Later, in September, Bragg would order Price and Van Dorn to march on Nashville.

At first it appeared that the invasion would succeed. Kirby Smith's army flanked Cumberland Gap, routed a Federal column at the battle of Richmond in Kentucky, and by September 1 had seized the state capital at Frankfort. Alarm bells pealed across southern Ohio, Cincinnati residents looked daily for Rebels, and Federal authority in Kentucky was a shambles.

To the south, meanwhile, Bragg forced Buell's army to abandon much of Middle Tennessee without firing a shot. On August 28, Bragg's army marched northward from Chattanooga. The gray column moved up the beautiful Sequatchie Valley to Pikeville and then drove north via Sparta, Carthage, and Gainesboro into central Kentucky.

Now it was Buell who was the hunted. Already the summer raids by Confederate horsemen had forced Buell to abandon his designs upon Chattanooga. Bragg then forced him to give up all of Middle Tennessee save for a garrison force at Nashville. Fearful of being isolated from his Louisville supply base, Buell literally raced Bragg into central Kentucky. Buell's fears proved to be short-lived. Supply problems, meager encouragement from Kentuckians, and poor cooperation between Bragg and Kirby Smith eventually doomed the great experiment. After a drawn battle on October 8 at Perryville, Bragg and Kirby Smith elected to retreat from Kentucky. Now the grand invasion became a long, dismal retreat across miserable roads in eastern Kentucky through the late October chill. Some Confederate units were desperately short of food, as they shepherded a long wagon train which included 20,000 rifles once intended for Kentuckians who never volunteered.

The failure of the campaign portended important matters for the future. Clearly the experience had taught that Kentucky was no Confederate state. More important, the high tide of Southern hopes had ebbed in the West. In matters of supplies and manpower, the Confederates had shot their proverbial bolt in the invasion. By 1863 the initiative would return to the Federals, who would become stronger as the Confederates steadily became weaker.

Yet there were some bright spots amid the blasted hopes of winning Kentucky. The bold stroke had cleared the Federals from most of Middle Tennessee, and Bragg was quick to take advantage of the situation. While Buell lingered in Kentucky, Bragg wisely moved into the Middle Tennessee bluegrass region. In November, after reaching Knoxville, Bragg's men were moved immediately into Middle Tennessee. On November 28, as an early snow pelted the surrounding cedar forests, the Army of Tennessee reached its new encampment along the Stone's River near Murfreesboro. Bragg's prompt move insured that, at least for the winter, the Rebels would control the fertile river valleys of lower Middle Tennessee.

The invasion of Kentucky had wrought another Confederate advantage. The Union ambitions on Chattanooga had been disrupted for almost a year. The previous summer, Buell's army had been within twenty-five miles of the prize. Now the Federals were at Nashville, the distance to Chattanooga was almost 150 miles, and the Army of Tennessee blocked the approach. Still, Bragg and his generals knew that the Federals would come again.

3. The Year of the War
for Chattanooga

The year 1863 would bring even harder war to the Tennessee country. Some of the Civil War's bloodiest engagements—Murfreesboro and Chickamauga—would be fought over the control of the Nashville-Chattanooga-Atlanta corridor. Simultaneously, Grant would advance from his bases in West Tennessee against the Confederate bastion at Vicksburg.

As previously mentioned, President Abraham Lincoln had three main strategic objectives in the Civil War, and two involved military operations in Tennessee—seizing the Chattanooga corridor and controlling the Mississippi River. In the late spring of 1863, a full-scale offensive by the Army of the Tennessee and the Army of the Cumberland would attempt these objectives.

Actually the campaign against the Chattanooga-Atlanta route began much earlier. After his retreat from Kentucky, Bragg positioned his army in the Murfreesboro vicinity. Intelligence reports were unusually scanty during late November and December, as Bragg's scouts had difficulty in penetrating a large Federal cavalry screen around Nashville. What Bragg did learn looked both grim and promising. The Federal Army of the Cumberland possessed 50,000 men at Nashville and could rely upon 30,000 reinforcements northward toward Louisville. And after Jefferson Davis in December ordered away reinforcements from Bragg to General John C. Pemberton's Vicksburg garrison, the Confederates at Murfreesboro could muster only 38,000 troops to oppose any invasion.

Still, Bragg and his lieutenants appeared confident that the Federals at Nashville would not advance until the spring. After all, the Lincoln administration, displeased with Buell's performance in Kentucky, had removed him from command of the Army of the Cumberland at Nashville. His successor, General William S. Rosecrans, later would prove to be a masterful strategist, but he possessed no such reputation in late 1862. In fact, Bragg and his generals were even a little contemptuous of the Federals at Nashville. Bragg in late December even speculated that Rosecrans might abandon Nashville and retreat into Kentucky.

There was another reason for overconfidence in the Murfreesboro camps. During the summer of 1862, Bragg had used cavalry raids to wreck Buell's advance on Chattanooga. In December the same pressure was applied against both Rosecrans and Grant, and it appeared to be successful. On December 7, General John Morgan's cavalry had swung northeast of Nashville, gobbling up an entire Federal brigade of over 2,000 men. In West Tennessee, four days later, General Nathan Bedford Forrest led four regiments on a spectacular raid against Grant's communications. Garrison after garrison was captured or routed at Lexington, Trenton, Humboldt, Union City, and elsewhere. Miles of track on the Mobile and Ohio Railroad were destroyed, fifty railroad bridges were burned, and 10,000 small arms were captured.

Finally Bragg sent his cavalry to operate directly against Rosecrans' supply line. On December 21, General John Morgan's command left the Lebanon area, penetrated Central Kentucky, and reached the Louisville and Nashville Railroad at Munfordville. Morgan wrecked the railroad from Munfordville north to within a few miles of Louisville and destroyed an estimated two million dollars in Federal property.

What Bragg did not know was that Morgan's celebrated "Christmas Raid" came too late. Throughout late November and December, Rosecrans had used the railroad to stockpile huge amounts of supplies in Nashville. Bragg only learned of this on December 20, when cavalry scouts penetrated the screen around Nashville. They reported another disturbing bit of news. If Bragg believed that Rosecrans planned a retreat into Kentucky, it appeared that he was in error. Rosecrans' three corps had been moved to the west bank of the Cumberland River.

It is to be suspected that a factor other than overconfidence caused Bragg and his generals to take lightly the threat of a Federal advance on Murfreesboro. The entire Confederate command structure on the western front was in turmoil, and it became a question of who was really in charge. On November 24, Jefferson Davis had revived the concept of theater command which he had used in 1861 with Albert Sidney Johnston. General Joseph Johnston had been recuperating from his wound suffered at Seven Pines and expected that he would be returned to the command of the Army of Northern Virginia. Even if Robert E. Lee's brilliant successes had not made this unreasonable, it is probable that Jefferson Davis would not have returned his bitter enemy to the post. Still, something must be done with Johnston. He was a ranking general, and his many political allies in Congress—most of them anti-Jefferson Davis men—demanded that he be given a command.

Davis responded by assigning Joe Johnston to a command which, on the surface, appeared to have vast authority. Johnston would command all territory between the Great Smokies and the Mississippi River: this included the major departments of Bragg in Tennessee and Pemberton in Mississippi, as well as the District of the Gulf, which embraced lower Georgia and Alabama and North Florida. The problem was that Johnston's authority was vague at best. Department heads would still report directly to Richmond, and not to Johnston. In effect, Johnston would not even know what was occurring in his command until he received second-hand news from Richmond. Johnston's relationship to commanders such as Bragg was equally cloudy. Johnston was empowered to go to any army headquarters within his jurisdiction whenever his presence was "necessary or desirable." Unclear was whether the government or Johnston would decide what was necessary.

By late December, as Rosecrans began to move against Bragg, the confused command situation had become apparent, Johnston was away from the Tennessee front when Rosecrans arrived. By December 21, he was in Mississippi, inspecting the Vicksburg fortifications. Actually, because of the faulty command structure, Johnston "lost" vast segments of his command during the Murfreesboro crisis. On December 27, he heard that Rosecrans was marching on Murfreesboro. Johnston did not even know if any reinforcements were available for Bragg in East Tennessee or at Chattanooga. Stevenson's division was somewhere en route to Pemberton's army—and was "lost" as well. So, too, was Forrest's cavalry command, still somewhere in West Tennessee.

Rosecrans could not have chosen a better time to advance. Weakened by the reinforcements sent to Mississippi, Bragg's army also lacked adequate cavalry. With Morgan and Forrest absent (a fact known to Rosecrans) Bragg's available troopers were hard pressed to do all that was required—to learn the routes of Federal advance, strike their communications, and screen the Confederate army. In November, Bragg had reorganized Army of Tennessee's cavalry into five brigades, and he had appointed General Joseph Wheeler as chief of cavalry. Small and cocky, the twenty-five-year-old Wheeler had not performed well in the Kentucky campaign. At several points, such as Munfordville, Bardstown, and Perryville, he had failed to provide good information as to the Federal lines of advance. Still, he was a favorite of Bragg's and must now perform his task with only three brigades—Morgan and Forrest were absent.

The nature of the geography around Murfreesboro required good service by the army's cavalry. Like spokes on a wheel, a number of roads radiated to the south and southeast from Nashville, by which Rosecrans could outflank Bragg if he desired. On the west, the Federals could advance on the good Columbia Pike via Franklin, or closer to Bragg, on the pike through Nolensville and Triune to Shelbyville. Polk and Breckinridge occupied the ground around Murfreesboro, while McCown's division was posted twelve miles east of Murfreesboro at Readyville. Wharton's cavalry brigade was almost thirty miles west of Murfreesboro at Franklin. By December 26, Bragg's army was stretched across a front more than forty miles wide.

And on that date, Rosecrans' corps smashed into this thin line. Bragg's army reeled back on Murfreesboro in confusion. Where was Rosecrans? He was reported on the Nashville-Triune-Shelbyville route, on the Nashville Turnpike at Murfreesboro, and on several other routes. Wheeler estimated that his cavalry brigades could slow Rosecrans enough to allow Bragg four days to concentrate his army. Bragg was grateful for the time and frantically drew his scattered detachments into Murfreesboro.

There was no good position at Murfreesboro. The town was surrounded by rocky fields interspersed with cedar groves. To the north of the town, a battle line could have been drawn up along the steep banks of Stewart's Creek. This would have covered only the direct approach via the Nashville Turnpike, however, whereas Bragg's intelligence reports on December 28-29 warned that Rosecrans was advancing on practically every road into Murfreesboro, from the Franklin Turnpike on Bragg's left flank to the Lebanon Turnpike on his right.

Only a battle line in the open fields slightly north of the town could cover all of these road approaches. And the position was further weakened by the peculiar course of Stone's River. Bragg's battle line was split in half by the river, which flowed north and then northwest on the northwest side of the town. Because of a peculiar bend in the river, the Nashville Turnpike and the Nashville and Chattanooga Railroad ran parallel to the river before crossing it into Murfreesboro.

By the morning of the twenty-ninth, Bragg had aligned his troops to meet a threat from any direction. Polk's corps occupied the fields west of Stone's River, stretching in a long semicircle from the river southwest across the Franklin and Wilkinson turnpikes. On the east bank of the river, Hardee's corps continued the line in semicircular fashion toward the Lebanon Turnpike.

But on the night of December 30, with skirmish fire already flaring on the battlefield, Bragg decided to shift his army's position. The previous night he had sent Wheeler's horsemen on a daring raid around Rosecrans' army and directed his cavalry chief to find Rosecrans. Wheeler's foray was little short of magnificent. He captured at least a thousand Federals and destroyed the entire supply train of General A.M. McCook —some 300 wagons. More important, Wheeler sent back important news—there was little Federal activity on Hardee's right flank in the Lebanon Road vicinity.

What was occurring was a curious procedure in which each commander planned an identical style of attack for the morning of December 31. Both Bragg and Rosecrans had planned to attack the other's left flank. Just as Polk was to roll forward at daylight, on the opposite side of Stone's River, General Thomas L. Crittenden's corps would fall upon Hardee. On December 30, Rosecrans had decided to mask Crittenden's assault by making a show of force on his right wing opposite Polk. Large numbers of campfires flickered through the cold, drizzling rain on Polk's front. Such maneuvers were enough to impress Bragg and his lieutenants that Rosecrans' heaviest concentration was on Polk's left flank, between the Wilkinson and Nashville turnpikes.

At a council of war on the night of the thirtieth, Bragg and his corps leaders decided to meet Rosecrans head-on. If he were concentrated opposite Polk, then Rosecrans would be attacked there. Almost all of Bragg's strength was now placed on the west bank of the river. General John McCown's reserve division extended Polk's original line to the Franklin Turnpike. General Patrick Cleburne's division of Hardee's corps was brought across the river to support McCown. This left only one of Hardee's divisions—Breckinridge's—on the east bank of the river.

Bragg's attack caught Rosecrans unprepared and almost wrecked the Federal army. At daylight McCown's division lurched forward, and soon the attack was taken up by Frank Cheatham's and Jones Withers' divisions of Polk's corps. The Federal right was held by General A.M. McCook's corps. By late morning, the hapless McCook watched as his corps was routed and driven back almost five miles to a position near the Nashville Turnpike. By noon the Federal line was at right angles. Crittenden's corps still faced eastward, opposite Breckinridge's men on the

---

Contemporary view of the battle of Murfreesboro. From *Harper's Weekly*.

east bank of Stone's River. General George Thomas' corps held the center at the critical angle, where Rosecrans' line then bent sharply northwest along the Nashville Turnpike. McCook's survivors continued the line along the pike toward Nashville.

The experience of Prentiss' division in the Sunken Road at Shiloh should have warned Bragg against headlong assaults against a strong position. Had Bragg reinforced and extended his flank, there appears little doubt that the Nashville Turnpike would have been seized and that most, if not all, of Rosecrans' army would have been captured.

Instead, Bragg and Polk concentrated against that portion of the line that would not give. At the angle where Rosecrans' line bent back toward Nashville, Thomas' corps occupied a strong position, protected by a deep railroad cut and by a four-acre stand of cedars on a stretch of high ground known as the Round Forest. Time and time again during the afternoon, Polk's men were ordered against the angle, only to be driven back by a murderous fire. Even Breckinridge's division was brought across the river during the afternoon and hurled against the angle. Confederate losses were ghastly. By the end of the day, Polk's corps was almost wrecked. Frank Cheatham's division had lost almost 40 percent of its strength, while Jones Withers' troops suffered almost 30 percent casualties.

A curious lull ensued on New Year's Day. Bragg had exhausted himself in beating Rosecrans. What was left to renew the fight? Polk's reserves were also a shambles. Cleburne's division of Hardee's corps had lost almost a third of its strength, and McCown's division from the East Tennessee army had suffered the loss of one-fourth of its strength. General Carter Stevenson's division—ordered away by Jefferson Davis—was missed sorely. Bragg's only fresh infantry was Breckinridge's 8,000 troops on the east bank of Stone's River.

Rosecrans also welcomed a pause in the battle. On the night of December 31, he and his corps officers had considered seriously a retreat to Nashville. Half-heartedly they elected to remain on the field but opposed attacking Bragg.

During the lull in battle on January 1, Rosecrans did make one significant change. When Bragg withdrew Breckinridge's division from the east bank of the river on December 31, he left unprotected some high ground just opposite Crittenden's corps on the Federal left. By the morning of January 2, part of Crittenden's force had crossed the river, seized the eminence, and now threatened to enfilade Polk's corps with an artillery crossfire. Bragg's attempt on January 2 to regain this position wrecked Confederate hopes of victory. Late in the afternoon, Breckinridge's division was sent forward to retake the slope. Instead, the Kentucky general's troops were met by massed artillery fire, and almost a third of the division was casualties.

Bragg now had no choice except to retreat. Losses were so heavy that only 20,000 Confederates could man the lines, and cavalry scouts warned of heavy enemy reinforcements. On the night of January 3, the Army of Tennessee began withdrawing from Murfreesboro. Four days later, the Rebels had taken up a new position along the Duck River. The new line promised to be a strong one. Bragg's men rested behind a high series of ridges which reached an elevation of a thousand feet. Still, the position was extremely wide because Bragg's troops covered lower Middle Tennessee from Columbia to McMinnville. The need to patrol this vast area was one reason why Bragg in early 1863 reorganized his cavalry into two large corps, under Generals Joseph Wheeler and Earl Van Dorn.

The creation of these large, mobile forces was also the work of the Western theater commander, General Joseph E. Johnston. Since the Richmond government insisted that both Bragg and Pemberton hold their positions and not join forces, Johnston pondered how each of them, greatly outnumbered, could resist Rosecrans and Grant. The general's solution was a system of "pipeline reinforcement." Van Dorn's cavalry corps was positioned in the Columbia-Spring Hill vicinity between Bragg's and Pemberton's commands.

During the winter and spring of 1863, both Van Dorn and Wheeler jabbed at Yankee supply lines. Van Dorn's destruction of Grant's Holly Springs base in December 1862 was no more spectacular than Forrest's West Tennessee raid that same month. Forrest's 2,100 troopers, crossing the Tennessee River at Clifton, played havoc with Grant's communications. By Christmas Day, Forrest had destroyed the Mobile and Ohio Railroad from Jackson to across the Kentucky border.

By 1863, however, the Confederates learned that Yankee riders could do the same thing. Gone were the earlier days when Federal cavalry was almost laughable with its inferior numbers, horses, and horsemanship. The decline of available Southern horseflesh, the work of the U.S. Cavalry Bureau in obtaining better mounts, the emergence of younger, more daring leaders—all combined to make a vast difference. In fact, one could argue that by the end of 1863, the cavalry situation had been reversed and that at least in manpower and horses, Union raiders were superior.

So, a curious war ensued in the country between Bragg's and Pemberton's armies. There were Confederate raids to halt Grant's forward move and Union responses to prevent interference with the Vicksburg expedition. There were Union thrusts deep behind Bragg's position, and Confederate counter-raids to force the recall of these expeditions. On occasion, there were even full-scale battles between whole divisions of cavalry.

Actually, most western Confederate raids in 1863 against enemy communications were ineffective. Lack of central planning, private ambition, and other matters combined to waste the opportunity to destroy either Grant's or Rosecrans' supply lines totally. After Forrest's and Van Dorn's successes of December, raiding became contagious. In February the ambitious young General Joe Wheeler talked Bragg into allowing him to attempt the recapture of Fort Donelson. The mission produced heavy Rebel casualties and damaged relations between Forrest and Chief of Cavalry Wheeler. Forrest swore he would never obey another order from Wheeler and thus was transferred soon to Van Dorn's cavalry division at Columbia.

General John Hunt Morgan also had the raiding fever. For most of early 1863, Morgan had been held in check by Bragg, who was irritated by poor discipline in the Kentuckian's brigades. Eager to regain his hero status, Morgan proposed a wild-eyed scheme to raid across the Ohio River, with a consequent march into Illinois or Pennsylvania. Bragg rejected the idea but did authorize Morgan to raid into Kentucky. On June 15, Morgan and almost 2,500 troopers left their camps near McMinnville and pushed into central Kentucky. Even before leaving Bragg's army, Morgan had confided to his brother-in-law, General Basil Duke, that he intended to disobey orders and cross the Ohio River. By July 8, Morgan was on the Ohio below Louisville, ready to cross into Indiana. His raid across the southern portion of that state and Ohio made good newspaper copy but was a military disaster. By August, practically the entire command had been captured, and Morgan's new headquarters was the Ohio State Penitentiary.

There were some bright spots. In March, Van Dorn's corps did repel two heavy reconnaissances from Nashville toward Spring Hill and Columbia. In one battle at Thompson's Station, north of Spring Hill, Van Dorn and Forrest pounded one invading column and bagged 1,300 prisoners. Another 1,800 Yankee horsemen were sent to Rebel prisons in April, after Forrest's command broke up Colonel Abel Streight's raid into North Alabama.

Still, as the summer campaign opened in Middle Tennessee, Bragg's cavalry was in bad condition. Morgan's command was lost north of the Ohio River. Van Dorn's command was broken up in May after that officer was murdered at his Spring Hill headquarters, allegedly by a jealous husband. Van Dorn's cavalry division was then returned to Mississippi. For the first time in the war, the Army of Tennessee's cavalry was outnumbered. By June of 1863, Bragg could muster only 8,000 troopers. Meanwhile, the able General David Stanley possessed over 12,000 cavalry on the Murfreesboro line.

If all of this were not enough to distract Bragg, certainly the army's command problems did so. Bragg's stay on the Duck River line, from January until June, was a miserable exercise in army politics. Bragg's sour disposition and habit of blaming subordinates for lost battles were always problems for the army's high command. Since the return from Kentucky, Bragg's camp had been plagued by one command crisis after another. In the autumn, Polk, Hardee, and Kirby Smith all had complained to the government that Bragg was a poor leader and should be removed. These complaints, along with a torrent of newspaper criticism and denunciations of Bragg on the floor of Congress, prompted Jefferson Davis himself to visit Bragg's camps shortly before the battle at Murfreesboro.

In early 1863, matters became worse. Bragg smarted under some criticisms of his retreat from Murfreesboro, and in January he addressed a famous "round robin" letter to his generals. In this incredible document, he asked their "candid" views of his capacity to command. The response of his generals was almost single-minded—Bragg should quit because he had lost the army's confidence. Bragg did not resign but instead launched a vendetta against various officers who he was convinced were undermining him. From January until May, the Duck River camps rocked with charges and countercharges by Bragg, Polk, Hardee, Breckinridge, Cheatham, McCown, and others. Three official government visits were made in an attempt to cool matters. In late January, Jefferson Davis ordered General Joe Johnston to Bragg's Tullahoma headquarters to ascertain what the problems were. Later, in March, Johnston was ordered back to Tullahoma and was authorized to replace Bragg and assume personal command. Still later, Jefferson Davis' aide, Colonel William Preston Johnston, was sent to the West to report on the troubles in Bragg's army.

The in-fighting had disastrous consequences. By June, morale was low among both officers and men. The corps leaders, Polk and Hardee, distrusted Bragg and considered him incompetent. Bragg himself was the most obvious casualty. The physical and mental strain had been too much, and by June he was near breakdown. Bragg's collapse soon became visible. On June 24, Rosecrans advanced from Murfreesboro with about 70,000 men. He feinted against Polk's position at Shelbyville but threw his strength against Hoover's Gap on Bragg's far right. By the morning of June 27, Rosecrans had pushed aside the feeble defenses at the gap, seized Manchester, and threatened to isolate the Confederates on the north bank of the Duck River.

Bragg's high command seemed unable to pull itself together long enough to fight Rosecrans. Bragg appeared dazed and unable to do anything but retreat. Hardee and Polk distrusted Bragg's judgment and in turn seemed unable to make a commitment to battle. Hardee even suggested that Bragg was too enfeebled to command and that the senior officers hold a secret meeting to discuss what should be done. Nothing was done. On July 2, after retreating successively to Tullahoma, Decherd, and Cowan, Bragg ordered a retreat to Chattanooga.

Rarely had so much precious ground been given up with so little fighting. Rosecrans had won Middle Tennessee—and at a cheap price. In the entire campaign the Federals lost only 570 men. Rosecrans had also gained the Cumberland Mountain range, the vital barrier on the road to Chattanooga. And since Bragg neglected to destroy the long Nashville and Chattanooga Railroad tunnel through the mountains near Cowan, the bluecoats had a good supply route for the future campaign against Atlanta. In fact, early July of 1863 was a bleak time for Southern hopes. Far to the northeast, General Robert E. Lee's army was falling back from Gettysburg. Meanwhile, to the southwest, Pemberton's army stacked arms and abandoned the Vicksburg fortress. With Pemberton's army gone and Vicksburg secure, Grant's army could now concentrate with Rosecrans against the Army of Tennessee. It was not long until the effects of Pemberton's surrender were felt. A third army had been created in Kentucky from General Ambrose Burnside's corps. The new Army of the Ohio, some 20,000 strong, had been intended for Grant's reinforcement. Now it was released for a campaign against East Tennessee.

By August 21, the invasion of the East Tennessee Valley had begun. The Confederate Department of East Tennessee had been abolished,

---

(*Above*): General Ambrose Burnside captures Knoxville in 1863. From *Harper's Weekly*. (*Below*): A photograph of Chattanooga during wartime. Courtesy of Tennessee State Library.

and its commander, General Simon Buckner, was now designated as commander of "Buckner's Corps" in Bragg's Army of Tennessee. On that date Buckner warned Bragg that Burnside's Army of Ohio was advancing toward Knoxville. Burnside bypassed the Confederate stronghold at Cumberland Gap and his army poured through nearby Big Creek Gap.

Buckner could do little to stop Burnside. His own small corps of 6,000 was outnumbered four to one. Instead, Buckner gave up Knoxville on August 24, abandoned the entire valley, and joined Bragg's army below Chattanooga. For the first time in the Civil War, the upper East Tennessee Valley was now in Federal hands.

Bragg was having his own problems. On August 21, the same day that Burnside moved on East Tennessee, Rosecrans advanced on Chattanooga. For a week the Confederates were fooled as to the Federal's destination. Rosecrans had decided to avoid a direct approach on Chattanooga. The logical roads for him to take from Middle Tennessee, such as the Anderson Pike and Haley's Trace, could be contested easily from the Confederate position. Rosecrans therefore sought to force Bragg to abandon the city without a fight. While a lone Federal brigade demonstrated in front of Chattanooga on the north bank of the river, Crittenden's corps approached from the west, along the road across the foot of Lookout Mountain. Meanwhile, the corps of Generals George Thomas and A.M. McCook marched far to the southwest and crossed the river at Stevenson and Bridgeport, Alabama. Rosecrans intended for these two corps to cross the mountains southwest of Chattanooga, move east, and cut Bragg off from Atlanta. Bragg must then give up the town, or be trapped between the Thomas-McCook column on the south and Crittenden's corps and Burnside's Army of the Ohio on the north.

Soon it became a question of who was stalking whom. Not until September 7 did Bragg pinpoint the location of Rosecrans' farflung corps. Rosecrans' strategy of sending two corps below Chattanooga while Crittenden's corps held Bragg at the town was good. Still, Rosecrans made one vital error. He divided the Thomas-McCook column, sending them on separate roads across Lookout Mountain.

Now the Federals were divided badly by both distance and terrain. McCook's column was at least forty-five miles southwest of Crittenden. The mountains of northwestern Georgia increased this distance. There was a successive wave of ridges to be crossed—Lookout, Pigeon, Missionary Ridge, and others—and the roads were almost intolerable. Bragg now saw his opportunity. He would concentrate against Thomas' corps when it emerged from the mountains, and Rosecrans' army would be cut in two. By the night of September 7, Bragg's troops began marching southward out of Chattanooga and took positions along the Chattanooga-La Fayette Road, on the east side of Pigeon Mountain. Twice within the next week, Bragg's army lost opportunities to defeat Rosecrans in piecemeal fashion. On the evening of September 9, Bragg learned that Thomas' advance had crossed Lookout Mountain into McLemore's Cove. The next day, Bragg sent several divisions into the cove to ambush Thomas. The movement was coordinated badly, and Thomas withdrew from the trap.

Now Bragg turned toward Chattanooga, hoping to demolish Crittenden's isolated corps. Before daylight on September 12, Bragg ordered Bishop Polk to march the eight miles from La Fayette, Georgia, to Crittenden's supposed encampment at Rock Spring Church. An incredible series of command delays ensued, Polk's command did not make contact with the enemy until the next afternoon, and Crittenden escaped.

Then a third opportunity was lost. By the evening of September 13, Bragg had concentrated almost 30,000 troops at Rock Spring Church. Crittenden's isolated corps was five miles distant, across Chickamauga Creek. Thomas' corps was ten miles away across Pigeon Mountain, and McCook was thirty miles to the south. Bragg was depressed and angry that his army had been unable to entrap the Federals. Now he gave up on the idea, withdrew his army to La Fayette, and allowed Rosecrans to concentrate.

Ironically, on the same day that Bragg fell back into a defensive position, Rosecrans finally realized his danger. He had not expected Bragg to fight near Chattanooga. When Bragg abandoned Chattanooga, he had left behind bogus deserters who infiltrated Yankee lines and told wild stories of how the Confederates were fleeing in panic toward Atlanta. Rosecrans had swallowed the bait, but now he knew the truth and desperately sought to concentrate his army.

By the evening of September 18, it was done. Rosecrans brought his three corps together in the valley of Chickamauga Creek, only about ten miles south of Chattanooga. The Union army rested in a north-south line along the Chattanooga-La Fayette Road. Behind the Federals was long Missionary Ridge, which formed the west rim of the Chickamauga Creek Valley. In their front was deep, meandering Chickamauga Creek, which flowed northeast toward Chattanooga. Bragg's lethargy had given the enemy a precious four days to unite the scattered corps. Now Rosecrans was ready.

For weeks, both sides knew well that the battle for Chattanooga was

taking place, and that the prize of victory was the gateway to Atlanta. In a rare mood of giving attention to the Tennessee front, Jefferson Davis had even authorized reinforcements from Lee's army in Virginia. When Rosecrans advanced in late August, Bragg warned the government that he was outnumbered badly. Rosecrans and Burnside had a combined force of about 95,000 troops against Bragg's 35,000 effectives.

What occurred in late August and early September was something rarely seen in Confederate operations—a concentration of force on a single line of enemy operations. From the Alabama-Mississippi theater, General Joe Johnston sent 9,000 infantry. From Lee's army in Virginia, the government ordered two divisions of General James Longstreet's corps to the western front. On September 9, fresh from the Gettysburg campaign, the divisions of Generals John Hood and Lafayette McLaws began leaving central Virginia for a union with Bragg. Much more aid could have been given. In Alabama, Johnston held back 16,000 troops which Bragg needed. And in Virginia, Lee's unwillingness to reinforce Bragg delayed the decision to send Longstreet. The government and Lee had been discussing such a reinforcement since late August. When Lee finally allowed the move, only two divisions were sent. Of these, only five brigades would reach Georgia in time to participate in the battle.

Bragg could not wait for Longstreet's arrival but now sought out the Federals along Chickamauga Creek. On the afternoon of September 18, the Confederates began forcing the ford and bridge crossings north of Lee and Gordon's Mill. By the morning of September 19, all Confederate units except for three divisions were positioned on the west bank of the stream. The resistance to these crossings on the eighteenth should have indicated to Bragg that something was wrong with his planning. All day on September 18 and well into the battle on the nineteenth, Bragg's view of Rosecrans' battle line was totally unrealistic. He believed that the Federal line was much farther south. Bragg's conception of the Union position placed Rosecrans' left wing, under Crittenden, at Lee and Gordon's Mill on Chickamauga Creek, with the right wing under McCook still farther to the south in the vicinity of McLemore's Cove.

Actually by the night of September 18, Rosecrans' left wing overlapped Bragg's right flank. Crittenden's corps was extended far beyond

(*Above*): Federal camps at Chattanooga. From *Harper's Weekly. (Below*): General Joseph Hooker's troops storming Lookout Mountain. From *Harper's Weekly.*

Bragg's northernmost crossing point at Reed's Bridge. And by September 19, Thomas' corps in the center also was positioned north of Lee and Gordon's Mill. Ignorant of Rosecrans' real position, Bragg on September 18 drew up an attack plan based upon the notion that the Federal left wing was at Lee and Gordon's Mill. Most of his army's strength was placed on the left and center, where he believed Crittenden's corps to be located. General Harvey Hill's corps was far to the south of Lee and Gordon's, and Polk's corps was in the center at the mill. Bragg's right wing, where he expected to deliver the flanking move, was the weakest position. Instead of seizing Rossville Gap and cutting off Rosecrans' from Chattanooga, Bragg intended for his left wing to cross at several positions north of Lee and Gordon's, turn southward, and overlap Crittenden's flank. A general attack would then be launched, driving Rosecrans into McLemore's Cove.

Another problem would arise when Bragg attacked on September 19. For months he had operated with the army organized into two large corps which were actually wings. Now he must attempt to fight a battle with a totally new command system. In August, Hardee had been transferred elsewhere, and his corps was now commanded by a former division leader in Robert E. Lee's army, General Daniel Harvey Hill. Hill was not the only new face in the Army of Tennessee's command. For all purposes, Bragg on September 19 was attempting to manage five separate corps. Aside from Polk's and Hill's units, there was Buckner's third corps, fresh from East Tennessee. Another corps, commanded by General W.H.T. Walker, was fashioned out of the reinforcements sent from the Alabama-Mississippi front by Joe Johnston.

By the afternoon of September 18, as Bragg was pushing across Chickamauga Creek prior to his attack next morning, a fifth corps was added. General John Bell Hood arrived on the field with several brigades of Longstreet's command. Hood was provided with a makeshift corps consisting of his own men and scattered detachments. A combination of ignorance of Rosecrans' position and such an unwieldy command system produced little success on September 19. The weakest portion of Bragg's line—the small commands of Hood, Walker, and Buckner—was to attack early in the morning and sweep southward against Crittenden's flank. Command confusion delayed the assault until noon, and when it surged forward, Bragg's right wing ran into a murderous fire from a Federal line that was not supposed to exist in that vicinity. For the rest of the day the battle disintegrated into a series of disjointed attacks delivered by Bragg's multitude of corps. Southern casualties were severe—

some divisions had lost one-third of their strength—and no ground of importance was gained.

On the night of September 19, Bragg attempted to patch his clumsy command system together. It was extremely cold that night, and a mixture of heavy smoke and fog hung over the shivering troops. While the exhausted army slept, Bragg fashioned a new, and equally unrealistic, command structure. Today he had fought with five corps. Tomorrow he would attack in two grand divisions. Bishop Polk would lead the right wing, while General James Longstreet would command the left. Bragg knew that "Old Pete" Longstreet had arrived that evening at Catoosa Station, on the Atlanta-Chattanooga Railroad line, and he was expected to reach Bragg's camp late that night.

The attack plans for September 20 were equally confused. Still Bragg did not understand that now he was overlapped on the north by Rosecrans, and Bragg clung to the strategy of driving in the Federal left wing and pushing the enemy back into McLemore's Cove. Polk's right wing would attack at daylight, and units on the center and left would then take up the battle. The problems were obvious. No special power was placed on the right wing, where Bragg still expected weak resistance. Worse, Harvey Hill's corps on Polk's far right flank was expected to begin the assault at Chickamauga at daylight. Since no unit could come into action until the force on its right attacked, it was essential that Hill attack promptly. But on the night of September 19 and the following morning, an almost comical chain of command blunders delayed the assault. Hill went to bed that night without knowing he was expected to move out at daylight. By the time the situation had been remedied, it was almost 10 A.M. Polk's attack ran headlong into Thomas' corps, which had been shifted to the left, and encountered Crittenden as well. For several hours, the battle reeled back and forth along the Chattanooga-La Fayette Road.

Until almost noon, Polk's men received no assistance from Longstreet. Longstreet was delayed by more than Bragg's insistence that the attack be taken up successively from right to left. Also, Longstreet had not reached his new headquarters until almost midnight on September 19, knew nothing of the terrain and less of the men he would command. In the early morning he was shocked to discover that whole divisions were misaligned badly and must be positioned properly before the left wing could attack.

When Longstreet did attack around noon, he discovered a pleasant surprise. Through a confusion of orders, a Federal division was withdrawn from the battle line, leaving a gap a quarter of a mile wide. Hood's men poured into the breach, and by 1 P.M. Rosecrans' right wing had collapsed totally. Panic seized McCook's and Crittenden's corps, and the troops fled to Chattanooga through gaps in Missionary Ridge. Even their commander was caught up in the rout. Rosecrans was much like Bragg—a superb strategist who became disoriented when under combat. At Chickamauga he panicked and fled for Chattanooga, leaving part of his army to its fate.

Fortunately for the North, that part left behind was commanded by Virginia-born George Thomas. When Thomas observed that the right and center had broken, he rallied his corps and some survivors of Crittenden's command. Thomas placed them on a steep, horseshoe-shaped elevation which protruded eastward from Missionary Ridge. Thomas hung on into the early evening and bought enough time for the bulk of Rosecrans' force to reach safety in Chattanooga. His line was at right angles, contesting Longstreet's and Polk's attacks simultaneously. In the mid-afternoon, it appeared that Thomas' men could not hold. About 3:30, Longstreet's wing launched a fierce new attack against one side of the Federal angle. Thomas gave ground, veterans of the charge at Gettysburg gained Horseshoe Ridge, and it appeared that the Federals would be swept away. At that moment, Thomas was saved by the appearance of the lead division of General Gordon Granger's reserve corps, which had been encamped northward on the road to Chattanooga. On his own initiative the resourceful Granger marched to the sound of the guns and threw his fresh troops against the fatigued Confederates. Wearily, Longstreet's men retreated back down the ridge. It was only a temporary victory. Outnumbered and suffering heavy casualties, Thomas must retreat. As dusk approached, Longstreet and Polk ordered a combined assault. The ridge line was carried, and Thomas' weary men fell back toward Chattanooga.

Chickamauga was a massive tactical victory for the Confederacy. A superior army had been defeated. Eight thousand Federals were captured on the field, along with almost 24,000 stand of small arms, fifty-one artillery pieces, and several tons of supplies. Rosecrans' total losses in the two-day engagement are still uncertain due to varying reports. A figure of 17,000 would be conservative. The Confederates had won the field but had done so at a frightful cost. The Army of Tennessee scarcely could survive many such victories. Bragg's casualties in the two-day fight were about 21,000, certainly at least 40 percent of his troops on the field. Twelve Confederate regiments lost half their strength in the bloodbath. Hood had lost his leg on the field, Hindman was shot in the face, and six of Bragg's brigade commanders were killed or wounded.

At first it appeared such heavy losses had at least won back Chattanooga. For two days after the battle, reports from the Chattanooga area told of a massive Federal retreat. Not until the morning of September 23, when the main body of the Army of Tennessee reached Missionary Ridge, did Bragg learn all of these reports were wrong. The Federals were not leaving but were erecting entrenchments around the south side of Chattanooga.

What should be done now? An attack upon Chattanooga appeared dangerous. The army could muster only 36,000 effectives; Rosecrans was believed to possess twice that number. Bragg instead decided to starve out Rosecrans. His intelligence sources reported that the Federal army had only six days rations. Moreover, the terrain on the south bank of the Tennessee River appeared to give Bragg control of most routes of supply into Chattanooga. Bragg arrayed his force in a six-mile semicircular line. Longstreet was given command of the left wing. It extended from atop Lookout Mountain and then down into the valley of Chattanooga Creek. In October, Hardee returned to the army and Polk was transferrred to the Alabama front. Hardee's line extended eastward from the creek valley and then along Missionary Ridge on the south side of the town.

Such a position did harass or seal off several supply routes. The deep river gorge in the Raccoon-Lookout Mountain area was impossible enough for steamboat traffic from Rosecrans' supply base at Bridgeport, Alabama. Longstreet's artillery atop Lookout made that route impossible. The Nashville and Chattanooga Railroad also extended from Rosecrans' base, but the Tennessee was vulnerable to Longstreet's artillery.

The key to starving out Rosecrans, however, lay in the area west of Lookout Mountain. From the mountain, Longstreet could gaze down into the valley of Lookout Creek and Raccoon Mountain beyond. Two roads from Rosecrans' Alabama supply base converged in the valley and crossed the Tennessee River at Brown's Ferry. One came up Lookout Creek Valley from Trenton, Georgia. A more difficult road led across Raccoon Mountain through Running Water Gorge. If the Federals could not open the Lookout Valley route, the only hope was to use a wagon road on the north bank which extended through sixty miles of rough mountain terrain before debouching into Middle Tennessee.

The Running Water Gorge road could be sealed easily enough by a handful of sharpshooters. But the main road up Lookout Creek was another matter. The valley was four miles wide there, and the road was out of range of Longstreet's artillery on Lookout Mountain. Nor could his guns reach Brown's Ferry, where the supply line crossed to the north bank of the river. It was essential that Longstreet place sufficient troops in the creek valley to block its use.

Longstreet never blocked the Lookout Creek route. In early October, he did send two regiments across the creek valley to dominate the northern end of Raccoon Mountain. But no force held the valley route from Bridgeport, even though Bragg and his general knew by October 28 that heavy Yankee reinforcements were en route to Chattanooga. Two corps of the Army of the Potomac were expected, as well as a large contingent of Grant's army in Mississippi.

One suspects that Bragg and his officers had become overconfident. The Federals at Chattanooga were suffering dreadful food shortages by early October and were forced to haul food along the tortuous mountain road across Walden Ridge and the Cumberlands. Rebel cavalry hammered away at the supply line. On one occasion Wheeler's troops bushwhacked and destroyed an entire corps' train of 800 wagons. What the Confederates did not destroy, the rugged terrain did. An estimated 10,000 mules and horses perished in the attempt to keep open a line of supply.

Perhaps the real reason why the Lookout Creek route was not secured was because the Confederates were too busy fighting among themselves. Another round of the old slugfest between Bragg and his generals erupted in the weeks after Chickamauga. Longstreet, Polk, and Harvey Hill even appealed to Jefferson Davis for Bragg's removal; twelve high-ranking generals petitioned the President to oust Bragg; and Davis himself was forced to hasten to the Chattanooga front to calm the situation. The consequence of this dispute was a total reshuffling of command. Davis sustained his old friend, and enemies of Bragg's such as Polk, Buckner, Hill, and even Nathan Bedford Forrest were sent elsewhere. Corps were restructured to separate anti-Bragg officers. Worse, relations between Longstreet and Bragg collapsed. Longstreet returned sullenly to his Lookout Mountain fortress and became a virtual recluse. Bragg and his left wing commander rarely communicated during October.

While Southern leaders fought among themselves, the Union army at Chattanooga was engaged in more constructive matters. On October 16, a new command organization was announced which eventually would bring disaster to the western Confederacy. General Ulysses S. Grant was appointed to command a new army group styled after the Military Division of the Mississippi. Now all three main Western armies—the Armies of the Tennessee, the Cumberland, and the Ohio—were to be concentrated against Bragg's army. And the concentration would be under Grant's personal leadership. By late October, events were moving swiftly. As soon as Grant was appointed, Rosecrans was relieved of command of the Army of the Cumberland. Grant hastened to Chattanooga and conferred with the new leader, the reliable General George Thomas. Sherman, who now had Grant's old command, was en route to Chattanooga with the Army of the Tennessee. General Joseph Hooker, with two corps from the eastern theater, was already at Bridgeport, ready to move.

Now the Lookout Creek route would be secured. First, Thomas must establish a bridgehead at the river crossing at Brown's Ferry. On the night of October 26, eighteen hundred troops floated on pontoons past Lookout Mountain and seized the ferry crossing. The next day, the small Confederate contingent on Raccoon Mountain was easily driven away. And by the afternoon of October 28, surprised Confederates on Lookout Mountain observed long lines of blue, as Hooker's men marched up the valley road and secured the river landing.

Longstreet made a half-hearted effort to regain a valley he should have held in the first place. A single Confederate division was sent into the valley on the night of October 28, 1863, to drive the Federals from the mouth of the valley. The ensuing "battle" of Wauhatchie, which occurred about 2:30 A.M., was a disaster. Longstreet's men were driven back to Lookout Mountain, and the Federals controlled the valley route.

Suddenly the fortunes of war had turned abruptly in favor of the Federals. At last foodstuffs could be brought to Thomas' hungry men and to the equally hungry civilian populace. A system of supply via steamboats, known as the "Cracker Line," was utilized. Since the river gorge beneath Raccoon Mountain was too difficult to navigate, boats halted short of the gorge at Kelly's Ferry. Supplies were then shipped by wagon across Raccoon Mountain to Lookout Valley, and thence to Brown's Ferry. Also, by October 29, Hooker's reinforcements from the Virginia army had reached the mouth of Lookout Valley. On November 20, they were joined at Kelly's Ferry by the advance of Sherman's Army of the Tennessee. In a few days, some 80,000 Federals were prepared to advance on Bragg.

The Confederates cooperated with Grant by dividing their army. Jefferson Davis had urged a diversionary attack upon Burnside's Army of the Ohio, encamped at Knoxville. The President believed such a move would force Grant to reinforce Burnside and weaken the army at Chattanooga. On October 31, Bragg met with his corps leaders—Longstreet, Hardee, and Breckinridge—to discuss how the Chattanooga situation could be salvaged. They agreed upon Davis' plan, even though they knew well that Sherman's Army of the Tennessee was already in Alabama en route to join Grant. Bragg desired that Longstreet lead the expedition—no doubt to be rid of one who had become a sworn enemy. Longstreet was as ambitious for independent command as he was desirous of leaving Bragg's company, and thus he heartily accepted the task.

The result of the division was that Bragg and Longstreet were defeated piecemeal. Longstreet's expedition to Knoxville was a disaster. After failing to ensnare Burnside at Lenoir's Station (Lenoir City) and Campbell's Station, Longstreet pursued the Federals to Knoxville. Outnumbered and facing a strongly entrenched foe, Longstreet still insisted upon an attack. After a week of confusion and uncertainty as to the objective, Longstreet hurled his men on November 29 against Fort Sanders, the northwest salient of the town's defenses. The assault, carried out amid rain and storms, was a disaster. Longstreet's men were repulsed with heavy losses, and the Knoxville campaign was over. Concerned by reports of approaching Federal reinforcements, Longstreet withdrew his two divisions into upper East Tennessee and went into winter quarters at Russellville. After a miserable winter, Longstreet's corps returned to the Virginia front. Their days on the Tennessee line were over.

Bragg's days in Tennessee were also ending. After Longstreet's departure, less than 30,000 Confederates manned the Chattanooga line. The line was so thin that the entire position from Lookout Mountain across to Missionary Ridge was manned by only two divisions. In effect, because of Longstreet's absence, Bragg uncovered his left and center and concentrated his two remaining corps—Breckinridge's and Hardee's—atop Missionary Ridge.

Grant wasted little time in hacking away at Bragg's thin line. On November 23, Thomas' Army of the Cumberland overran Orchard Knob, Breckinridge's advance position in the valley. The following day, Hooker's 10,000 troops marched out of Lookout Creek Valley and assailed Stevenson's division on Lookout Mountain. Actually the defenders could muster scarcely more than a brigade to defend the heights. By 3 P.M., Stevenson's entrenchments were carried, and his troops were withdrawn across the valley to Missionary Ridge. By the morning of the twenty-fifth, Bragg was reduced to the Missionary Ridge position.

The end of the long campaign for Chattanooga came on November 25. Grant's huge army now moved to destroy what remained of Bragg's army. From Missionary Ridge, the Confederates saw activity during the day in all directions. On the west, Hooker's corps moved slowly up the Chattanooga Valley to outflank the ridge position. In the center, Thomas' army moved steadily toward the left and center of Bragg's ridge position. Meanwhile, Sherman's army moved against Bragg's far right, where the railroad to Knoxville tunneled beneath the mountain.

Grant intended for Sherman's army to assail the northeast sector of the ridge and carry Bragg's right flank, while Thomas and Hooker attacked simultaneously on the center and left. Sherman's plan was stalled by a magnificent defense by Cleburne's lone division, which held off the Federals for the entire day. On the west, Hooker had difficulty in traversing the Chattanooga Creek Valley and did not strike the west end of the ridge as Grant had planned.

It remained for Thomas' troops to win the battle of Missionary Ridge. Serious alignment problems existed on Bragg's left and center, held by Breckinridge's corps. Breckinridge's lines were already thin because Bragg had massed Hardee's corps on the right, where he feared an attack from Sherman. Then Breckinridge's troops were placed in three lines of rifle pits—at the base of the ridge, halfway up the slope, and on the ridge itself. Such a formation threatened disaster if troops in the most advanced line of rifle pits were compelled to fall back suddenly. Atop the crest, Bragg's engineers had complicated matters by placing the last line of entrenchments too far back from the ridge crest. It was thus possible for an enemy to approach within a few yards of the ridge fortifications without being seen. Above all, Bragg's problem was simply a lack of manpower. Longstreet's departure had eroded the army's strength badly. On November 25, it is doubtful that Bragg had 26,000 men available to man the ridge position.

The break in the line came suddenly, after Cleburne's division on the right flank had held Sherman at bay throughout the afternoon. About four o'clock, Thomas' army swept forward and overran the line of works at the base of Missionary Ridge. Then, without orders, Thomas' men did not halt but scrambled up the steep slopes and fell on Bragg's second line. When it collapsed, Confederates now fled toward the ridge position, pursued hotly by Thomas' men. Atop the ridge, gray soldiers in the last line could scarcely fire, for fear of hitting their retreating comrades. Suddenly, panic swept Breckinridge's corps, and Thomas' attack turned into a Confederate rout. Thousands of small arms were thrown away by the panicked troops, and forty pieces of artillery were seized or abandoned. With Cleburne's division fighting a magnificent rearguard action, the remnants of Bragg's army fell back along the Atlanta railroad. By November 28 the Army of Tennessee had reached Dalton, Georgia, where it would go into winter quarters before the spring campaign of 1864.

Braxton Bragg would not be with the army. After the Missionary Ridge disaster, which included the loss of 6,000 men, the cry was raised again for Bragg's removal. Worn by over a year of command turmoil, Bragg could command no longer. On November 28 he penned his resignation and five days later left the army.

Confederate fortunes had changed radically since the early autumn of 1862. It had been a little more than a year since Bragg and Kirby Smith had pushed toward the Ohio River, while Robert E. Lee's banners waved north of the Potomac.

Now the high tide of Rebel fortunes had ebbed. Lee's hopes for the one grand stroke which would end the war had been blasted by the three-day carnage of Gettysburg. President Abraham Lincoln's determination to regain control of the Mississippi River became a reality with the surrender of Pemberton's Vicksburg garrison. Confederate hopes of foreign recognition were now feeble. The military defeats were enough in themselves. But President Lincoln's Emancipation Proclamation in January of 1863 had given the war a broader purpose than the restoration of the Union. Now it was a war to banish forever human slavery from North America.

And in North Georgia, the defeated veterans of the Chattanooga campaign awaited the final onslaught. The erratic but brilliant Rosecrans had forced open the Nashville-Chattanooga corridor, and the stubborn, realistic General Ulysses Grant had secured the approach to Atlanta. Grant's victories at Chattanooga were a beginning, but the waves of bluecoats and the mountains of supplies gathered in the river town portended an end.

4. The Last Hard Year of War

Now it had come, that slow, grinding nature of Federal military victory. The old style of the Civil War was gone by 1864. There were still battle flags, regimental bands, and cavalry units which possessed an air of romance, but the war was more a managerial exercise in which Federal soldiers by the hundreds of thousands were arrayed in the main war zones on the Tennessee and Virginia fronts.

Since early 1862, most of Tennessee had been a Federal encampment, a staging area for the long campaign against the Atlanta corridor. Little remained of the romance that had accompanied the enthusiastic gray-clad legions which had volunteered in 1861. Gone were the lunches of fried chicken served to young volunteers, the admiring glances flashed by young ladies, and the inevitable orations by incumbent politicians. Instead, when Bragg's losses at Chattanooga opened the Atlanta front to invasion, the war on the western front became one of management— how many railroad cars were needed to supply Sherman's combined army group, how many hospitals were required in Nashville, and where would the Federal quartermasters locate the tons of supplies which Sherman needed.

Even by 1862 the war had changed Tennessee's landscape abruptly, particularly in major cities and towns. For two years after Nashville was surrendered to General Don Carlos Buell's advance units, the capital had become an impregnable fortress and was one of the most strongly fortified cities in the country.

The entire Nashville character had been changed by the war, and perhaps never would be the same. South of the city, the once-pleasant terrain between the Hillsboro and Nolensville Pikes was a maze of earthworks and fortified positions. Spacious ante-bellum mansions had been seized as Yankee headquarters or hospitals, and fashionable lawns had been denuded of trees for fortifications and firewood. Typical was Longview, out on the Franklin Pike. The spacious grounds had been

stripped of trees, and ugly military barracks dotted the lawns. Belmont, the stately home of Joseph Acklen, was occupied by the Federals, and its water tower was a lookout post.

Certainly the environmental shock was awesome and involved more than the fact that hundreds of fine Tennessee homes had been converted into Federal command or hospital installations. Hundreds of miles of railroad track had been destroyed, and the debris of war was everywhere. The bleached bones of horses still lay on battlefields such as Shiloh and Murfreesboro. Fortifications cut huge gashes through sections of Chattanooga, Knoxville, Columbia, Nashville, and dozens of other locales.

There was the social change which perhaps had more impact. By 1864 the entire state of Tennessee was an army camp, and the cultural shock was obvious. Shortages of food, clothing, and medicine were grave. Ersatz became the order of the day. Instead of coffee, residents of Dyersburg or Morristown drank substitutes of dried sweet potatoes, peanuts, or okra. Pies baked in Cleveland, Pulaski, and Jackson contained little sugar, but only honey or sorghum when available. The ink used by a Union City resident to write a letter now came from berries, and the stationery could be a scrap of wallpaper.

Everywhere there were hardships. Within months after Nashville fell, the citizens were faced with shortages of common items. By the end of 1862, for example, the price of potatoes had soared to four dollars a bushel, firewood cost twelve dollars a cord, and sugar gradually was non-existent.

The residents could have accepted such privations more easily had the social structure remained the same. Instead, because of their positions as Federal staging areas, Tennessee's communities were subjected to a state of flux which few other Confederate states were forced to endure so long. Thousands of newcomers flocked into Memphis, Nashville, Chattanooga, Knoxville, and elsewhere as soon as the Confederates retreated. Many were prostitutes, gamblers, and misfits who fed from an army of occupation. For example, in early 1863, of a population of 35,000 people, some 19,000 inhabitants of Memphis were listed as "newcomers." Among these new residents in Memphis and elsewhere were the prostitutes; by 1863 the editor of a local newspaper complained that the city had become the "great rendezvous" for pimps and ladies of

---

(*Above*): The Tennessee State Capitol in 1864. Courtesy of Tennessee State Library. (*Below*): Scene at a Federal military hospital in Nashville, at mid-point of the war. Courtesy of Tennessee State Library.

the evening. Nashville could do little better. Hundreds of prostitutes came to Nashville, and the reported rate of venereal disease among Federal troops averaged twenty-eight men a day by late 1863. Once that same year the prostitute rate in Nashville became so severe that a boatload of 150 of the worst offenders was shipped northward to Louisville and Cincinnati. The ladies were unwelcome there too, however, and were returned to Middle Tennessee.

From Knoxville to Memphis and from Chattanooga to Clarksville, the civilian population suffered the effects of hosting an army of occupation. Prostitution, gambling, and public drunkenness were only the tip of the proverbial iceberg. Shortages of food, clothing, and commodity items were the order of the day. Churches were hospitals; railroad bridges were destroyed; restaurants swarmed with swaggering Yankees; and once gentle cornfields were filled with discarded wagons, dead horses, broken artillery pieces, and the graves of soldiers.

Tennesseans were now suffering from being in the backwater of the Civil War. Since 1861 the state had been on the front line of battle, but when the great Federal offensive began in May of 1864, the war shifted to Georgia.

After defeating Braxton Bragg in the Chattanooga campaign, General Ulysses S. Grant was *the* supreme hero of the Union, the man who had achieved two of Abraham Lincoln's war objectives—the opening of the Mississippi River and the seizure of the corridor to Atlanta. In March of 1864, Grant was given control over a third objective: the defeat of General Robert E. Lee's Virginia army. Grant was summoned to Washington as commander of all Federal armies, and his close friend General William Sherman took charge of Federal armies on the western front.

During March and April as the defeated Army of Tennessee regrouped at Dalton, Grant and Sherman fashioned a strategy which eventually brought defeat to the Confederacy. While a smaller army under General Nathaniel Banks would exert pressure on Alabama and Mississippi, Sherman would march south from Chattanooga, drive back the Army of Tennessee, and seize Atlanta. Meanwhile the Federal Army of the Potomac (with Grant as supervisor) would move against Lee while a secondary force threatened the Richmond-Petersburg area.

On May 4 the great Federal campaign began. In the East, the well-equipped veterans of the Army of the Potomac crossed the Rapidan River. And in the West, a long trail of 100,000 bluecoats streamed out of Chattanooga across Missionary Ridge and into Georgia.

Within four months Confederate hopes on the western front were a shambles. The North Georgia and Atlanta campaigns were a slow, dismal bloodbath which resulted in at least 40,000 Confederate casualties, the loss of the vital rail center at Atlanta on September 8, and the destruction of tons of Rebel supplies.

Amid the disastrous campaign, the Western Confederate army had suffered as well a radical change of command. After Bragg left the army in December, a public cry went up for the appointment of General Joseph E. Johnston. The small, cocky Johnston may have been an enemy of Jefferson Davis, but he was immensely popular with the Southern public. After a barrage of newspaper editorials and congressional speeches, President Davis relented and appointed Johnston.

Johnston and Davis shared such a mutual hatred that command accord was impossible. During the long retreat from Dalton to Atlanta, Johnston refused to explain his motives to the President, and Davis in turn ignored the problems which "Old Joe" faced in the West. So on July 17, on the eve of the Atlanta campaign, Johnston was removed from command, and General John Bell Hood was appointed to lead the Army of Tennessee.

A young, blond-haired Kentuckian, Hood had garnered quite a reputation as a hard-fighting division commander in Lee's Virginia army. Then came two wounds which surely affected him deeply. At Gettysburg, his arm was shattered badly and rendered useless; soon after, his leg was amputated on the field at Chickamauga. During the autumn of 1863, while recuperating in Richmond, Hood yearned to regain an important field command. He ingratiated himself with Jefferson Davis and by 1864 was telling the President what he wished to hear—that the Confederates in the West should attack Sherman. Clearly, Hood's theme was that victory in Georgia was possible, if the right man led the Army of Tennessee.

Jefferson Davis was impressed with such bravado and in early 1864 sent Hood to the western front as a corps commander in Joe Johnston's army. Immediately Hood began a secret—and illegal—correspondence with Davis and other Richmond officials which labeled Johnston as an incompetent officer who was not willing to fight Sherman. The combination of Hood's letters and rising discontent in Richmond with Johnston resulted in the change of command on July 17. Within two and one-half months, Hood promptly lost four major engagements and the prize of Atlanta.

What would the Western Confederates do now? By late September,

Hood's decimated Army of Tennessee lay at Palmetto, about twenty-five miles west of Atlanta. Meanwhile Rebel intelligence warned that Sherman planned to move soon, toward either the Gulf or the Atlantic. Hood's losses had not diminished his fighting spirit. Once at Palmetto, Hood was smitten with new dreams of glory. The Confederates possessed only 23,000 infantry to match Sherman's nearly 100,000 men at Atlanta and almost that many again along the railroad to Louisville. Hood reasoned correctly that he could do little save retreat if he remained at Palmetto.

The problem was that his ambitions soon outweighed practical considerations. Hood's strategy in subsequent weeks changed radically from a simple design to shift to the north of Atlanta and threaten Sherman's communications into an all-out invasion north of the Ohio River. By late October, Hood had talked the Richmond government into accepting his scheme, and his army lay at Florence, Alabama, far to the northwest of Atlanta. Hood's scheme to recapture Nashville and drive across the Ohio River did not take into account the realities of Federal strength. After a brief pursuit of the Confederates toward the Alabama border, Sherman had retired to Atlanta. But unknown to Hood, Sherman had enough men both to march to the sea and to stop the Rebel threat. In late October, General George Thomas had been sent to Nashville to cope with Hood's threat. With reinforcements from Missouri and two corps from Sherman in Atlanta, Thomas could rely upon 70,000 men to resist Hood. Ironically, Hood at Florence was unaware that such an army was being organized to stop his invasion threat.

In late November, amid freezing weather, Hood's army marched northwest from Florence into Middle Tennessee. Now his march on Nashville would become a race. Hood's intelligence told him little of any forces at Nashville under Thomas. But he did know that General John Schofield was at Pulaski, Tennessee, with the 23rd Corps and part of General David Stanley's 4th Corps. Both the Federal and Confederate routes to Nashville converged on Columbia. From Florence, Hood's men must march seventy miles via Waynesboro, Lawrenceburg, and Mt. Pleasant to Columbia. There they would intersect Schofield's line of march. From Pulaski, Schofield had only a thirty-mile march to Columbia.

The Federals won the race to the Duck River crossing at Columbia. Schofield reached Columbia on November 24. That same day, Hood's advance—Forrest's cavalry division—fought hard to drive Schofield's men back from the Duck River crossing. From November 25-27, Schofield concentrated his two corps at Columbia and frantically began throwing up fortifications. But as Hood approached the army's main body, the Federals abandoned the works on the night of November 27 and retreated to the north bank of the Duck River.

There was a new spirit in the air when the Army of Tennessee reached Columbia. They were back home in the rich Middle Tennessee bluegrass, a far different sight from the dreary red clay country from Chattanooga to Atlanta. Tennessee was home for the majority of Hood's army, and most of his men had not even set foot in the state since Bragg was driven out of Tennessee by Rosecrans. On the night of November 27, 1864, high spirits pervaded a meeting of Hood's generals at his headquarters on the Pulaski Pike. The falling snow and bitter cold did little to dampen spirits. Hood now believed he possessed the initiative and intended to use it. So he unfolded a bold plan to his corps officers— Generals Frank Cheatham, Alexander Stewart, and Stephen Lee.

Hood evidently saw Nashville as an unguarded city. He intended to win this prize by flanking Schofield and beating the Federals in the race. This could be done by a bold flanking maneuver. On November 29, Cheatham's, Stewart's, and part of Lee's corps, covered by Forrest's cavalry, would cross the Duck River upstream from Columbia at Davis' Ford. Two of Lee's divisions with the army's artillery and trains would provide a hearty demonstration to hold Schofield on the north bank of the river opposite Columbia. Meanwhile, the main Confederate column would advance via the Davis' Ford road the thirteen miles to Spring Hill and then seize the main pike to Nashville.

The ensuing command fiasco at Spring Hill on November 29 has been enshrouded both in myth and confusion. After the war, in the "Lost Cause" era of Confederate war history, ex-comrades would become bitter against one another and seek any instance of misconduct in the war in efforts to damage an officer's reputation. The same Lost Cause mentality demanded "might have been" situations, where, but for a single quirk of fate, victory would have belonged to the Confederates.

The episode at Spring Hill became part of the Lost Cause mythology. Decades of writers would both accept the old tale and embellish it. When it was done, Spring Hill became one of the war's decisive encounters. Hood, aiming to cut Schofield off from Thomas' army at Nashville, skillfully outflanked him. Hood possessed the opportunity to destroy Schofield's army completely. But he fumbled the opportunity, and Schofield was allowed to retreat on to Franklin within the light of Confederate campfires.

The first strategic blunder by Hood was his flanking march to Spring Hill, designed not to encircle Schofield but to bypass him and hurry on to the Tennessee capital. Also, Hood did not win the mythical race to Spring Hill. On the morning of November 29, Forrest's cavalry divisions, followed by Cheatham's and Stewart's corps, began crossing the Duck River at Davis' Ford, upstream from Columbia. Forrest was slowed in reaching Spring Hill because he was first required to drive back Schofield's cavalry, which was positioned on the Franklin-Lewisburg Pike. Not until shortly before noon did Forrest reach the village of Spring Hill.

By then the village was occupied by two garrison regiments, and General David Stanley was approaching with General George Wagner's infantry division. By 2 P.M., Wagner's infantry, nearly 6,000 strong, held a very strong position on the high ground around Spring Hill and was supported by Schofield's entire reserve artillery corps. During the afternoon, only Cheatham's corps—barely 6,000 infantry—reached Spring Hill. Due to command confusion and marching on unfamiliar roads, Stewart's corps was not in position until at least eight o'clock that evening. By seven o'clock, Schofield had two large divisions and his reserve artillery at Spring Hill, with another two divisions approaching the village from the south.

During the afternoon, there had been sporadic attempts by divisions in Cheatham's corps to move against the Federals occupying Spring Hill. Command confusion was rampant, and there were contradictory orders sent by corps leader Frank Cheatham and by Hood. One suspects that Cheatham and his division commanders were unsure exactly what the objective was. To Hood, the objective was not Schofield's troops in the village but winning the race to Nashville. For example, when General A.P. Stewart came up with his corps, he was not pressed forward into any assault on Spring Hill. Stewart was told to bivouac his men and to resume the march toward Nashville the next morning. That night Hood boasted that he had won the race. He obviously miscalculated how rapidly Schofield could march from Columbia to Spring Hill and appeared confident that Schofield's army would not reach the village before November 30.

During the night, at midnight and at 2 A.M., Hood received only two reports that Schofield was actually in motion on the pike to Nashville. While his subordinates must bear some responsibility for not giving him full information, Hood's reaction to these reports was also lethargic. Whether from exhaustion or other reasons, Hood did little save to order a single regiment to move to the pike and fire on any passersby. Hood was enraged when he learned on the following morning that Schofield's troops had passed during the night. Obviously he was too emotionally distraught to continue in command. He lashed out at Cheatham and his division commanders for failing to seize the road to Nashville and lamented that one of the war's great opportunities was lost. Exhausted, sick, and emotionally unstable, Hood was a shell of the fine young division officer who had crossed the Potomac with Lee in the Gettysburg campaign.

Hood now became totally unreasonable. Although General Stephen Lee's corps and the army's artillery were still at Columbia, Hood was determined to hunt down and destroy Schofield. The hunt ended in the early afternoon. Schofield halted at Franklin and awaited Hood's advance. Franklin, located in a curve of the Harpeth River, was a natural fortress on the north, west, and east. On the south side of the town—Hood's approach—the Federals since 1862 had maintained a long set of earthworks which extended from the river above the town to near the river below Franklin. These were no ordinary earthworks: there were deep outside ditches, headlogs atop the dirt parapets, and a menacing array of abatis and *chevaux-de-frise* to slow an enemy's advance.

Such an advance must come across two miles of rolling, open ground. From Winstead Hill, a ridge south of the town, the land leveled into an open plain stripped of trees during the long Federal occupation. An attack on Schofield's position would subject the Confederates to a murderous artillery fire both from Schofield's guns in the earthworks and from the massed artillery across the river at Fort Granger. An assault on such a position would have been madness.

Hood reached Winstead Hill about 2 P.M. and instantly ordered the army to prepare for a frontal assault. His subordinates protested. Only 19,000 infantry were available because two of General Stephen Lee's divisions were not up. There was no artillery support to soften the Federal position. Also, an assault was unnecessary. Forrest knew the country well because of his long stay there in 1863. He tried to convince Hood that the army could cross the Harpeth River upstream from Franklin and flank Schofield out of Franklin. Hood would not be dissuaded. Cheatham's and Stewart's men were aligned along the ridge slopes on both sides of the Columbia Pike. At 4 P.M. the signal was given to advance, and the long battle line weaved forward unevenly.

It was the last great spectacle of the old style of war, played out long after the vaunted Pickett-Pettigrew charge at Gettysburg. Eighteen infantry brigades in battle formation marched across the bluegrass plain. Regimental bands played, tattered battle flags lifted in the breeze, and coveys of quail fled the approaching Confederates. Down Winstead Hill, across the Harpeth River plain, they marched to within a half-mile of Franklin. Now the bands stopped while the columns shifted into two long battle lines. The signal came, and thousands of yelling Confederates lurched forward.

Immediately the geography of the Harpeth River plain proved disastrous to Hood's attack. When the Confederate line was first formed, out on Winstead Hill, it was three miles wide, stretching from the Carter's Creek Pike on the west, across the Columbia Pike to the Lewisburg Pike on the east. The curvature of the river soon constricted this space. As the three roads converged on Franklin, the battle front was narrowed into a space only a half-mile wide.

This constriction of the Confederate line produced two fatal effects. It meant that those elements of Cheatham's corps moving along the Columbia Pike in the center of the line—the divisions of Generals Patrick Cleburne and John C. Brown—would strike the Federal line before the Confederate left and right would reach the earthworks. Stewart's corps on the right and those divisions of Cheatham on the left were forced to halt and readjust their lines as the field narrowed.

Meanwhile, Cleburne and Brown had been repulsed in the center. The main line of Federal entrenchments was open at the Nashville Pike, but a barricade across the road and artillery massed at the Carter House made the gap in the breastworks a veritable trap. Cleburne and Brown had first overrun two brigades of Wagner's division which had been posted along the Columbia Pike about a half mile in advance of the breastworks. The Federals had fled pell mell up the Columbia Pike and through the gap in the main fortifications. The Confederates poured into the breach, and fighting raged through the grounds of the Carter House. A furious hand-to-hand fight occurred around the Carter House and a cotton gin across the road. Then Federal reserves rammed into Cleburne's and Brown's weary troops and pushed them back through the gap. While Cleburne and Brown were driven back, the remainder of Hood's infantry met a galling artillery fire as they neared the breastworks. Whole regiments could neither advance nor retreat, and they huddled in the ditch on the outside of the parapet as Federal small army and artillery continued a murderous fire.

Despite the heavy casualties, Hood continued to press the attack and even sent reinforcements from Lee's corps into the holocaust. Finally, about 9 P.M. the firing died down, and the Confederates in the outer ditch drifted back to count their losses. Meanwhile, Hood—both emotionally drained and ignorant of the real situation—planned to assault the works again at daylight.

There would be no more attacks because the army had been almost destroyed. Only about 16,000 infantry had actually gone into action, and 6,200 were casualties. Of these, 1,750 had been killed in five hours of combat—more battle deaths than the Federals had suffered at such two-day engagements as Chickamauga and Shiloh, or in other bloody battles of Chancellorsville and Stone's River. Losses among officers were equally staggering. Six generals had been killed, five were wounded, and one was captured. Fifty-four regimental commanders were killed, wounded, or captured. Losses were especially severe in those divisions that had fought along the Columbia Pike. General Patrick Cleburne and one of his brigade commanders were killed. General John C. Brown was wounded, and all four of his brigade commanders were casualties. After the battle, a colonel was the ranking officer in Brown's division. Even after the arrival of Lee's corps, Hood now possessed fewer than 18,000 infantry.

Still Hood pushed on grimly to Nashville. After the war, Hood would state that he knew that General George Thomas had gathered a large army at Nashville. Hood maintained that his plan had been to take a defensive position south of the city, await reinforcements, and then compel Thomas to attack him. A close survey of Hood's correspondence in 1864 indicates this was hindsight. There is little evidence that he knew that Thomas, with the addition of Schofield's force, now had an army of 70,000 men in Nashville.

If Hood did know of Thomas' strength, as he asserted after the war, then his troop dispositions did not indicate this fact. As his army approached the city, Hood sent off an infantry division and two cavalry divisions under Forrest—6,500 men—to the Murfreesboro area. This left Hood with only 15,000 infantry to conduct his "siege" against a powerful enemy behind twenty miles of breastworks in one of the most strongly fortified cities in the country. In an effort to control at least some of the many roads which led south from Nashville, Hood established a paper thin line. By December 8, only 15,000 men held a line five miles long, stretching from the Hillsboro Pike on the west, across the Franklin Pike to the Nolensville Pike.

On December 8, Hood faced another enemy. The mercury plunged that night to ten degrees, and sleet and snow pelted his poorly clad troops. By the next day the Nashville area was covered with ice and snow, and the many barefoot men in Hood's army suffered severely. The ground was frozen hard, and it was impossible to complete the line of earthworks Hood had envisioned.

By the middle of the month it was obvious that Hood was in a trap. Certainly the army could not assail the powerful Nashville fortifications. It was equally certain by then that the army could not retreat. Hood's wagon transportation was broken down completely. Too, it would be extremely hazardous to attempt a withdrawal in the face of such an overwhelming Union force. If this were not enough, a sudden thaw had melted the ice and snow, and the roads south of Nashville were quagmires of mud. It became almost impossible to move either wagons or artillery.

General George Thomas had been waiting for this thaw. For two weeks, the War Department and General Grant had badgered Thomas to march out of his entrenchments and attack Hood. Thomas had demurred, insisting first that his cavalry lacked adequate mounts and later that the icy weather prohibited such a move. Finally Grant lost patience and on December 13 dispatched General John Logan to Nashville to assume command. Grant was so concerned that on December 15 he left his headquarters on the Richmond-Petersburg siege lines and prepared to go in person to Nashville.

Neither Logan nor Grant reached Nashville. On that day, Thomas hurled his troops against Hood's weak position. While a feint was made on the Confederate right, the hammer blow came against the Rebel left wing along the Hillsboro Pike. Waves of blue infantry, supported by General James Wilson's massive cavalry corps, overlapped Hood's left and overran his redoubts along the Hillsboro Pike. By 4:30 P.M., as dusk approached, the battered remnants of Hood's left wing streamed westward toward the Granny White Pike.

There was little time to form a strong defensive position. Hood's new battle line, two miles to the south of his position earlier in the day, was extremely weak. He deployed the army in the Brown's Creek Valley, on the north side of the massive Overton Hill range. Lee's corps held the right flank, anchored on Peach Orchard Hill, just east of the Franklin Pike. In the center, Stewart's corps extended the line westward to the Granny White Pike. Cheatham's line on the left flank extended several hundred yards west from the pike to the crest of Shy's Hill, where it bent back abruptly.

Obviously Hood was fooled by the Federal demonstration on December 15 against his right flank. Much of the army's power—Lee's and much of Stewart's corps—was aligned on the right flank. The weak element was Cheatham's corps and the peculiar angle in his corps' line as it bent southward from Shy's Hill. Unknown to Hood, Thomas had massed two corps on Cheatham's front, aligned in a right angle facing the vulnerable Shy's Hill position. Thomas' plan for the fight on December 16 remained the same—to threaten Hood's right flank along the Franklin Pike while throwing the Federal strength against the left.

At 9 A.M. on the sixteenth, Thomas' left wing surged forward against General Stephen Lee's position along the Franklin Pike. The fight evolved into more than a mere feint against Hood's right; it was a bloody affair which centered upon Lee's right anchored along Peach Orchard Hill, at today's intersection of the Franklin Pike and Battery Lane. Meanwhile, the corps of Generals John Schofield and A.J. Smith were pressing hard against Cheatham's beleaguered troops at the angle on Shy's Hill. Early in the morning, Federal artillery began a fierce bombardment. One Federal battery alone discharged almost six hundred rounds against Cheatham's position that day. Through the early afternoon, as a cold drizzle fell, the cannonade continued.

Finally, the end came at about four o'clock. Schofield had ordered an all-out advance on the right angle of Cheatham's line. From the Hillsboro Road region, Schofield's 23rd Corps poured across the Sugartree Creek Valley, while Smith's 16th Corps advanced through the hills bordering modern-day Lone Oak Road. Meanwhile, General James Wilson's huge cavalry corps flanked Cheatham on the southwest, moving along the general route of present-day Tyne Boulevard to attempt to seize the Granny White Pike behind Cheatham's position.

Within a few minutes, the war on the western front had ended. Cheatham's position atop Shy's Hill, held by the division of General William Bate, collapsed, and the remnants of the Confederate left wing fled for the Granny White Pike. When Cheatham's men gave way, so did the Confederate center under General A.P. Stewart, positioned between the Granny White Pike and Lee's troops near the Franklin Pike.

The retreat soon became a rout. Artillery, small arms, and equipment were strewn aside in the attempt to flee Thomas' overwhelming numbers. General James Wilson's Federal troopers held the Granny White Pike in Cheatham's rear, occupying a strong position in Granny White Gap, just south of the present-day Tyne Boulevard. When Cheatham's men realized that this escape route was sealed off, the panic increased, and they fled across the fields east of Granny White Pike toward the

Franklin Pike. General Stephen Lee's corps held on until the other two Confederate corps could reach the Franklin Pike. Then, too, they were forced to fall back hurriedly, losing sixteen artillery pieces in the melee.

Hood was now fleeing for North Alabama and the shelter of the south bank of the Tennessee River. Whether he could reach safety was questionable. Confederate losses in the two-day battle exceeded 6,000, and the army now could scarcely muster 10,000 infantry in condition to fight. There was little artillery remaining, since fifty-four guns had been lost on the field. The Franklin Pike was strewn with small arms, equipment, and personal belongings. Meanwhile, thousands of General James Wilson's Federal cavalry, with excellent mounts, stormed at the rear of Hood's retreating column.

Once again, General Nathan Bedford Forrest exhibited the skill which had made him one of the South's most respected soldiers. At Murfreesboro, Forrest realized that a disaster had occurred, and he drove his troopers hard across country to meet Hood's column. On December 19 he joined the army at Columbia and took charge of the rear guard. At Columbia, Hood gave Forrest charge of a mixed command of 5,000 cavalry and infantry to hold off the Federals until the army could get across the Tennessee River.

The last days of December became a nightmare for the Army of Tennessee. The weather had changed again, and a new winter storm caused much suffering. The ice brought by the earlier storm had been melted by the thaw of December 13. Now the pools of water in the dirt roads were frozen hard, and thousands of Confederates, literally barefoot, suffered terribly. Through Columbia, Pulaski, and across the Alabama border, Forrest's column held off Thomas' pursuit. Daily the rearguard column was forced to fight off the Federal pursuit. There was even a stiff encounter on Christmas Day in the hills south of Pulaski.

Finally Hood reached the shelter of the south bank of the Tennessee River. On December 25-26, the main body of the army crossed at Bainbridge, Alabama. At the same time, the army's last engagement on western soil was fought on Sugar Creek. Again Forrest's rearguard beat back Wilson's troopers in a skirmish fought across snow and ice. On the night of December 27, Forrest's rearguard began crossing the Tennessee River on a pontoon bridge which had been captured from the Federals

---

A Federal hospital in Nashville at the close of the war. Courtesy of Tennessee State Library.

in North Alabama. By December 29, the last of Forrest's men were across.

Except for isolated skirmishes, the Civil War had ended on the Tennessee front. Hood's force—less an army than a remnant of one—regrouped at Tupelo, Mississippi. While the army still possessed about 15,000 infantry, less than half this number were considered effectives. Most of the army's artillery was gone, there was little food and no winter clothing, and the wagon transportation had been destroyed.

Destroyed as well was the once mighty Army of Tennessee. After a broken General John Bell Hood was relieved from command in late January, the balance of the Army of Tennessee was transported to the Carolinas in a desperate attempt to halt Sherman's march northward toward Virginia. In the Carolinas, they were united with remnants of the Carolina Department and were placed under the command of General Joseph Johnston.

This last-ditch effort had no hope of success. Johnston did give Sherman's left wing a hard fight at the battle of Bentonville, North Carolina, on March 19, but the end was near. On the early morning of April 11, Johnston was awakened at his headquarters near Raleigh and was informed of the surrender of General Robert E. Lee's army in Virginia. Now Johnston's army—about 21,000 men—would be confronted by almost a quarter of a million troops under Sherman and Grant. There was no other choice but to surrender.

On April 26, 1865, it was done. The Army of Tennessee, veteran of combat in every Confederate state east of the Mississippi River except Virginia and Florida, was surrendered. The Confederacy was gone. With the surrenders of Lee and Johnston, other Southern armies soon laid down their arms.

Now they would come home to Tennessee, these mere remnants of regiments that had volunteered with such boyish enthusiasm in 1861. There was the Fourth Tennessee Infantry, for instance, a West Tennessee regiment that had been organized in 1861 at Germantown. Then it had numbered almost a thousand men. After four years on the western front, it mustered only a few dozen. The Fourth Tennessee had fought

---

(*Above*): War scene on the East Tennessee and Virginia Railroad, near Strawberry Plains. Courtesy of Brady-Handy Collection, Library of Congress. (*Below*): Chattanooga railroad yards during the war. Courtesy of Library of Congress.

at Shiloh, had marched with Bragg into Kentucky, and had returned to suffer at the battle of Murfreesboro. The regiment's odyssey was a lengthy one. It was with Bragg in the disaster at Chattanooga, with Joe Johnston in North Georgia, and with Hood in Middle Tennessee. When the end came at the battle of Nashville, the Fourth Tennessee journeyed to the Carolinas and surrendered with General Joe Johnston.

And when the war was no more, the regiment began the long march across the Smoky Mountains to Nashville, where they boarded steamboats for West Tennessee. En route, the survivors halted in Asheville, North Carolina, and unfurled the old battle flag which had been made four years earlier by some ladies in Montgomery, Alabama. Tearfully, the men folded the flag, trudged through the mountains to Greeneville, Tennessee, and climbed aboard a train for Nashville.

Now they were almost like ghosts from the past, even though the bitter trauma of the Lost Cause would endure for generations. How different Tennessee must have appeared to them! The hated Andrew Johnson was no longer the state's military governor. Now he was the President of the United States, President because only weeks before, Lincoln had been cut down by an assassin's bullet at Ford's Theatre. Johnson had been placed on the election ticket in 1864 because Lincoln had sought a coalition of moderate Republicans and Union Democrats. Now he resided in the White House, the East Tennessee unionist who had been so despised by the cotton and tobacco planters west of the Cumberland Mountains.

The train rattled toward Nashville. The bridges along the East Tennessee railroads had been rebuilt now, and the fiery unionist guerilla activity of 1861 was in the past. The scars of war were evident at Knoxville and Chattanooga, yet the bustle of activity and factory smoke spoke of the new order.

The new order was also there at Nashville, when the veterans of the Fourth Tennessee stepped from the train. Civilian control had been returned to the state, and in March the former abolitionist William G. Brownlow had been elected governor. Brownlow was no friend to ex-Rebels. Already he had recommended to the legislature that the fran-

---

(*Above*): William G. Brownlow, prominent East Tennessee Unionist. Courtesy of Tennessee State Library. (*Below*): An issue of Brownlow's newspaper, the *Knoxville Whig*. Courtesy of Special Collections, University of Tennessee Library, Knoxville.

BROWNLOW'S KNOXVILLE WHIG,
AND REBEL VENTILATOR.

VOLUME I.   KNOXVILLE, TENN., WEDNESDAY, JANUARY 11, 1865.   NUMBER 49.

The Knoxville Whig.

W. G. BROWNLOW, Editor.

Knoxville, Tennessee, Jan. 11, 1865.

Personal.

Immediate Emancipation.

Defence of Dr. Cawood.

Carped on British Intrigues.

THE PRINTER AND I.

BY QUINTILIA G. OTON.

John Mitchell on Fools.

TO THE PEOPLE OF JEFFERSON COUNTY.

chise be offered only to Union men, and he had pushed through the legislature an act which provided a $5,000 reward for the arrest of former Governor Isham Harris.

Isham Harris had fled to Mexico along with a number of other ex-Rebels. Zollicoffer was long dead after the shots fired in the pelting rain at Mill Springs. Dead also were Bishop Polk after a chance shot during the North Georgia campaign, Albert Sidney Johnston in the Peach Orchard at Shiloh, and Pat Cleburne after the holocaust at Franklin. Jefferson Davis was in chains, the Kentuckian John C. Breckinridge was paddling through Florida swamps en route to Cuba and England, and General P.G.T. Beauregard drifted back to New Orleans.

The men of the Fourth Tennessee, whether they realized it, must have been an anachronism as they moved along Broad Street in Nashville toward the river landing. The ugly scars of Federal occupation were everywhere, but the town already had begun to recoup the old commercial bustle of the pre-war years.

The air was balmy—far unlike the snow and ice of the Nashville campaign—as the ex-Rebels boarded steamboats for West Tennessee. Down the Cumberland they went, past the old earthworks at Fort Donelson, past the vanished powder mills that had churned out gunpowder for Beauregard's men at Bull Run. Then the boats reached the Ohio River and headed downstream for the junction with the Mississippi.

They were moving now past the old bastion at Columbus, Kentucky, and at Island Number Ten. Then the sluggish craft began moving into tiny river landings, and steadily the veterans lumbered down the gangplanks onto the West Tennessee shore. At landing after landing they shouted hoarse goodbyes and then disappeared into the flatlands. The war was over in Tennessee.

Suggested Readings

Even though it was neglected for years, the western front in the Civil War now boasts an ever-growing body of writings. A short monograph such as this requires only a basic list of readings on the Civil War in Tennessee, and for a complete bibliography, readers may wish to consult the sources listed in two volumes by the author, *Army of the Heartland* and *Autumn of Glory.*

Irving A. Buck. *Cleburne and His Command,* ed. Thomas Robson Hay. 2nd ed., Jackson, Tenn., 1959.

Mary Campbell. *The Attitude of Tennesseans Toward the Union, 1847–1861.* New York, 1961.

Thomas Connelly. *Army of the Heartland: the Army of Tennessee, 1861-1862.* Baton Rouge, 1967.

————. *Autumn of Glory: The Army of Tennessee, 1862-1865.* Baton Rouge, 1971.

————. and Archer Jones. *The Politics of Command: Factions and Ideas in Confederate Strategy.* Baton Rouge, 1973.

John P. Dyer. *"Fightin' Joe" Wheeler.* Baton Rouge, 1941.

Gilbert Govan and James Livingood. *A Different Valor: the Story of General Joseph E. Johnston, C.S.A.* New York, 1956.

————. *The Chattanooga Country, 1540-1961: From Tomahawks to TVA.* New York, 1952; 3rd ed., Knoxville, 1977.

Robert Hartje. *Van Dorn: the Life and Times of a Confederate General.* Nashville, 1967.

Thomas Robson Hay. "Braxton Bragg and the Southern Confederacy," *Georgia Historical Quarterly,* IX (Dec. 1925), 267-316.

————. *Hood's Tennessee Campaign.* New York, 1929.

Ralph Selph Henry. *"First with the Most" Forrest.* Indianapolis, 1944.

Stanley Horn. *Army of Tennessee.* 2nd ed., Norman, Okla., 1955.

————. ed., *Tennessee's War, 1861-1865, Described by Participants.* Nashville, 1965.

_____. *The Decisive Battle of Nashville.* Baton Rouge, 1956; rpt. Knoxville, 1968.

Nathaniel Cheairs Hughes, Jr. *General William J. Hardee: Old Reliable.* Baton Rouge, 1965.

Robert J. Johnson and Clarence C. Buel, eds. *Battles and Leaders of the Civil War.* 2nd ed., 4 vols. New York, 1956.

Archer Jones. *Confederate Strategy from Shiloh to Vicksburg.* Baton Rouge, 1961.

James Lee McDonough. *Shiloh—in Hell before Night.* Knoxville, 1977.

Grady McWhiney. *Braxton Bragg and Confederate Defeat,* vol. I, *Field Command.* New York, 1969.

Joseph Howard Parks. *General Edmund Kirby Smith, C.S.A.* Baton Rouge, 1954.

_____. *General Leonidas Polk, C.S.A., The Fighting Bishop.* Baton Rouge, 1962.

Charles Roland. *Albert Sidney Johnston: Soldier of Three Republics.* Austin, 1964.

Glenn Tucker. *Chickamauga: Bloody Battle in the West.* Indianapolis, 1963.

T. Harry Williams. *P.G.T. Beauregard, Napoleon in Gray.* Baton Rouge, 1955.

John Allen Wyeth. *That Devil Forrest: Life of General Nathan Bedford Forrest.* 2nd ed., New York, 1959.

Index

Tennessee Three Star Books

Visions of Utopia
Nashoba, Rugby, Ruskin, and the "New Communities"
    in Tennessee's Past
by John Egerton

Our Restless Earth
The Geologic Regions of Tennessee
by Edward T. Luther

Tennessee Strings
The Story of Country Music in Tennessee
by Charles K. Wolfe

Paths of the Past
Tennessee, 1770–1970
by Paul H. Bergeron

Civil War Tennessee
Battles and Leaders
by Thomas L. Connelly

Tennessee's Indian Peoples
From White Contact to Removal, 1540–1840
by Ronald N. Satz

THE UNIVERSITY OF TENNESSEE PRESS : KNOXVILLE

DATE DUE			
FEB 1 2	*King*		
OCT 2			
OCT 4			
DEC 2 0			
JAN 1 4			
FEB 1			
APR 2 2			
APR 3 0			
SEP 4			
OCT 1 0			
DEC 9			
FEB 1			